"God has blessed Gateway Church with explosive growth. Pastor Robert Morris humbly unpacks many of the invaluable lessons he and his team have learned along the journey. His spiritual insight and practical instruction will help you build a stronger, deeper, and broader ministry."

—CRAIG GROESCHEL, senior pastor
of LifeChurch.tv and author of *Soul Detox:*
Clean Living in a Contaminated World

"I've had the privilege of seeing 'behind the curtain' at Gateway Church and can honestly say that this church is way more impressive from the inside than it is from simply looking at it on the outside. Pastor Robert Morris has done a tremendous service to God's kingdom by sharing the Gateway story in *The Blessed Church* and helping us understand that the real issue we should focus on is church health. What you will gain from reading this book is not only inspiration but also principles that will work in any church (or business) that wants to fully maximize its potential."

—PERRY NOBLE, founding and senior pastor
of NewSpring Church

"Our world desperately needs healthy, vibrant churches, so I'm thankful Robert Morris has written *The Blessed Church*—a book that draws on the Gateway backstory to describe the qualities of a healthy local church. More than anything, a heart for God and a love of people define the ministry of Pastor Morris and Gateway Church. If you want a growing vitality in your church, you will profit from every page of *The Blessed Church*."

—CHRIS HODGES, senior pastor of Church
of the Highlands

"A healthy church grows—and so do its people! Gateway Church is such a place. In *The Blessed Church,* Pastor Robert Morris tells how any church, regardless of size, can become a thriving spiritual haven for both shepherd and sheep."

—JOHN C. MAXWELL, author and speaker

"In *The Blessed Church,* Robert Morris reveals why Gateway Church in Dallas–Fort Worth has become not just one of the largest churches in America but also one of the most influential. Robert's devoted, attentive shepherding of this great flock is one reason why Gateway is so blessed. In *The Blessed Church,* the biblical principles that lead to true success in the body of Christ are carefully explained. If you love the local church, as both Robert and I do, you won't want to miss the insights found in this helpful and practical book."

—DR. TONY EVANS, senior pastor of Oak Cliff Bible
Fellowship and president of The Urban Alternative

"When I refer to the blessed church, I am speaking from firsthand experience. My wife, Betty, and I are active members of Gateway Church, which Robert Morris pastors. We have witnessed and experienced the dynamic power and profound impact made on personal lives, families, the community, the church at large, and the nation. The blessed church members live a blessed life and continually seek to be a blessing to others. Through Pastor Morris's leadership, Gateway Church has become a model and inspiration to the whole church around the world. Your church can experience the bountiful blessings of our God and Father right here on earth right now!"

—JAMES ROBISON, founder and president of LIFE
Outreach International and co-host of *LIFE Today*

"Robert has put together a master playbook for victory in the church. Every pastor can learn from the insight and wisdom God has given Robert and the Gateway team. In fact, I truly believe that practicing the biblical principles of health and growth outlined in *The Blessed Church* will help us all further the Great Commission and experience radical transformation and blessing in our communities."

—Tom Mullins, founding pastor of Christ Fellowship Church

"Every pastor, layman, leader, and churchgoer should read *The Blessed Church*. Morris has done it again. Readable and inspiring, *The Blessed Church* is a must-read for all who want their own church to walk in the blessings of God."

—Mark Rutland, PhD, president of Oral Roberts
University and Global Servants

"The story of Gateway Church is one of radical trust, bold vision, and the faithfulness of God. Now my friend, Robert Morris, has written a book telling that extraordinary story. Read it! You will realize that God wants to bless your church more than you ever could have imagined."

—Greg Surratt, senior pastor of Seacoast Church

"I've been close friends with Robert Morris for more than twenty years, and when Gateway started, I mentored Robert closely and taught him what I knew about church government, leadership, and other relevant issues. Robert was and is humble, teachable, and uncompromising in doing things God's way. In my opinion, this is the main reason for God's blessing upon Gateway Church. *The Blessed Church* is a must-read for anyone wanting to know how to build a church that God will bless."

—Jimmy Evans, senior elder of Trinity Fellowship Church
and CEO and founder of MarriageToday

The
Blessed
Church

Other Books by Robert Morris

The God I Never Knew
The Blessed Life
From Dream to Destiny
The Power of Your Words

The Blessed Church

The Simple Secret
to Growing the Church You Love

ROBERT MORRIS

WATERBROOK
PRESS

THE BLESSED CHURCH
PUBLISHED BY WATERBROOK PRESS
12265 Oracle Boulevard, Suite 200
Colorado Springs, Colorado 80921

ISBN 978-0-307-72973-6
ISBN 978-0-307-72974-3 (electronic)

Library of Congress Cataloging-in-Publication Data
Morris, Robert (Robert Preston), 1961–
    The blessed church : the simple secret to growing the church you love / Robert Morris.
        p. cm.
    ISBN 978-0-307-72973-6—ISBN 978-0-307-72974-3 (electronic)
1. Church growth. I. Title.
    BV652.25.M68 2012
    254'.5—dc23
                        2012022353

Printed in the United States of America
2012—First Edition

10 9 8 7 6 5 4 3 2 1

SPECIAL SALES
Most WaterBrook Multnomah books are available at special quantity discounts when purchased in bulk by corporations, organizations, and special-interest groups. Custom imprinting or excerpting can also be done to fit special needs. For information, please e-mail SpecialMarkets@WaterBrookMultnomah.com or call 1-800-603-7051.

This book is dedicated to Bill Hybels, who has exemplified to me a Blessed Leader and Blessed Church. He continues to walk in humility, transparency, integrity, and determination to turn irreligious people into wholly devoted followers of Christ!

~~~

Bill, I'm grateful for our friendship and the personal times you have spoken into my life. Even if we had never had a single face-to-face meeting, your life, example, teaching, and writing still would have inspired me to live my life a certain way and to stir others to do the same: to nurture a wholehearted passion for Jesus and people, and to keep His bride healthy so she can have the greatest impact!

Contents

PART 4: BLESSED LEADERS

PART 5: BLESSED GOVERNMENT

PART 6: BLESSED CHURCH CULTURE

Introduction

To the best of our ability, we have built Gateway Church on principles that have brought God's blessing on us so that we might reach and disciple more people—who in turn will reach others. I'm writing this book to share these principles, because I desire to do everything in my power to build God's kingdom through His local church.

What I have tried to clearly address in this book are the principles upon which healthy churches are built. I speak from the reference of Gateway Church because that's where I serve, not because I believe it is the only or the healthiest. We are continuing to learn from many others in the body of Christ. I'm so grateful we're laying down our swords and picking up our plowshares to work together!

A while back, Pastor Jack Hayford and I were speaking to some pastors when all of a sudden Jack said, "You guys are asking the wrong questions! You keep asking Robert *how* Gateway does this and that! You need to be asking him *why*. What's the principle behind the policy?"

That comment made me stop and think. Had I been guilty of telling young inquiring leaders of integrity *how* I do it but not *why* I do it? Had I focused more on the methods than the motives, the actions rather than the attitudes, and the head rather than the heart?

When I began writing this book, I gave it the title *Healthy Things Grow*, because I believe with all of my heart that spiritual health is the key to church growth (and when I say church growth, I mean reaching people who don't know

Christ and discipling them to do the same). God's blessing brings spiritual health, and spiritual health brings God's blessing. I believe we need to understand the *how-tos* of church growth, but more importantly, we must also understand the *whys*.

This book has been a collaborative project incorporating the insights of many on Team Gateway. Foremost among them is my dear friend and Gateway's executive senior pastor, Tom Lane. Tom has been searching God's Word, praying, and thinking deeply about biblical models of church governance and administration for most of his adult life. He is an amazing gift to the body of Christ, to our church, and to me personally. And he has graciously made the riches of his wisdom and insights fully available to this work.

One of our founding elders, Steve Dulin, has contributed his insights and anecdotes, as have many of Gateway's key staff pastors, including an associate senior pastor, Thomas Miller (Gateway's original and lead worship pastor), and another associate senior pastor, David Smith. Indeed, I got pretty much the entire staff involved in this project, asking them for their insights, perceptions, and stories.

Please read this book with an open heart and mind. You will undoubtedly find things you would say differently, outright disagree with, or don't wholly relate to you, but don't write off the rest. These principles are based on my understanding of Scripture and are being put to the test every day. It is my sincere desire that God will give you some insight—some revelation—that will take you much further than I have and that together we will plunder hell and populate heaven! May we pastor churches that God blesses to be a blessing!

> To you first, God, having raised up His Servant Jesus, sent Him to *bless*
> you, in turning away every one *of you* from your iniquities. (Acts 3:26)

PART ONE

The Gateway Story

1

God's Story, Not Ours

Short of being a passenger on a rocket ship to Mars, I was about as far away from my North Texas home as a man could be. I had just finished speaking at a pastor's conference in Australia when a young minister from New Zealand approached me with a question. It was a familiar one: "What's the key?"

He didn't have to elaborate. I was pretty sure I knew what he meant. But I encouraged him anyway.

"The key to what?" I responded.

"Gateway's growth. I mean, what in heaven's name is going on up there? What are you guys doing?"

He was referring to Gateway Church, the fellowship that it's my privilege to pastor. The "what's going on" at the heart of his question has been an ongoing story of astonishing growth and rising influence.

How astonishing? Well, Gateway began with a handful of friends in a living room Bible study back in 2000. As I write today, the church sees more than twenty thousand people participate in live worship and teaching each weekend. The growth has been steady, dramatic, and shows no sign of slowing down. On the pages that follow, I hope to reveal why I think we've experienced the blessings we have.

Nevertheless, I confess that I've had to work through some feelings of reluctance and awkwardness about writing this book.

That's because the last thing we—myself or any of our team—would ever want to do is appear to be bragging or patting ourselves on the back. The very thought of anyone saying "Who does that guy think he is?" makes me want to shrink back and count my blessings in grateful silence. But the Lord won't allow it.

The fact is, I don't think I'm anything special. And of all God's people, I'm the most aware that what we have experienced over the last twelve years has absolutely nothing to do with any smarts, special talents, or abilities I might possess.

On the contrary, I might be the most unlikely candidate you'll ever meet. But that's God's MO, isn't it? He chooses the rustic, barely educated fisherman Peter to carry the gospel to the cream of Jewish society. And He sends Paul, with his elite education and sterling religious pedigree, to pagan Gentiles who couldn't care less about his Jewish credentials.

Thus, I'm not a walking advertisement for the church-growing power of natural talent, clever strategy, and brilliant marketing. I'm a living, breathing testament to the power of God's unfathomable grace.

Nevertheless, it's impossible to deny that God has done something remarkable at Gateway Church. Wherever we go, I and members of our team are asked about it. Those questions take a variety of forms:

- "What's your secret?"
- "To what do you attribute your church's amazing rate of growth?"
- "How did you become one of the largest and fastest growing churches in America in just a few short years?"
- "How have you been able to remain balanced, healthy, and focused while riding a virtual rocket sled of increase?"
- "How do you identify, develop, and/or attract leaders to your cause?"

It is to bring clear answers to these questions in a spirit of transparency, humility, and gratitude that I have finally undertaken this book. Frankly, God will not let me off the hook.

In the end, the Lord has made it clear that He wants the Gateway story told because it's *His* story—not because we've done everything right, but rather because He has accomplished something special *in spite of* our weaknesses and mistakes. He wants these principles shared because they're *His* principles. And the church bodies scattered across planet Earth by the tens of thousands are *His* too. He wants to see them healthy, growing, influencing, and overcoming.

So on the pages that follow, I'll share what we've learned and what I've seen in the Word. Not because I have all the answers, but because I have *some* answers. A few of them may surprise you. Thus, throughout this book you'll find little nuggets of truth and insight labeled "Keys to a Blessed Church."

To begin, I will share a brief overview of how I came to found Gateway Church and the amazing journey of grace and favor we have been on over the last dozen years. I'll follow that by sharing the spiritual principles, biblical precepts, school-of-hard-knocks lessons, and surprising insights that have made that journey so extraordinary.

2

Hearing from God

I GREW UP A REBELLIOUS, SIN-ATTRACTED BOY in a wonderful Christian home. But when the Lord got hold of me at the age of nineteen, His grip of grace was firm and unbreakable.

Very soon after my dramatic salvation experience—*too* soon in retrospect—I entered ministry as a youth evangelist, preaching and speaking all over the country. Paul offers some clear warnings about thrusting young believers into high-profile ministry positions too quickly (see 1 Timothy 3:6). Nevertheless, I loved the Lord, sensed His call, had a burning heart for souls, and committed myself to serve Him for the rest of my life.

That led to Bible college and then ultimately a ministry staff position at a wonderful, Spirit-filled church in Grand Prairie, Texas: Shady Grove Church, led by a wise and gifted man of God, my friend and spiritual father, Olen Griffing.

I had served there under Olen's leadership in a variety of roles, including evangelism pastor, for more than a decade. At the ripe old age of thirty-one, I was the father of three young children; I was happy, content, and fruitful. Then one day Olen and I were riding in a car together when out of the blue he mentioned something that would change my thinking and ultimately the course of my life.

He mentioned that he knew he couldn't serve as senior pastor of Shady Grove forever and that one day—in perhaps three to five years—he'd want to retire. To my surprise, he said he wanted me to know that he viewed me as the most likely candidate to succeed him when that day came. He encouraged me to add that prospect to my thinking, praying, and preparation for the future.

I can tell you with complete truthfulness that serving as the senior pastor of any church, not to mention Shady Grove, had never entered my mind before that day. My assumption had always been that if the day ever came that the Lord called me away from Shady Grove, it would surely be to return to traveling evangelism.

Of course, after I arrived home, I immediately told my wife, Debbie, about the surprising conversation. In fact, she noted it in her journal that night. The next morning in my quiet time, I asked the Lord directly about it: *Lord, is this what You have for me? To be a senior pastor of a local church someday?*

I didn't ask about Shady Grove specifically. Before I heard from Him about my future at Shady Grove, I needed to hear from Him about the broader issue of what it was I was called to be.

Yes, Robert, was the reply that I heard from the familiar voice in my spirit. And then He said something else.

Before I tell you what it was, you need to understand that I have always had the type of relationship with the Lord in which I hear Him very clearly. When I attune the ear of my heart to His voice, He speaks to me very precisely and with great detail, just as my wife or any other intimate friend of mine speaks.

If this seems odd to you, please also understand that this ability is not a gift reserved for a few special prophets. The ability to hear the voice of God is the birthright of every believer. (This book is not the place to elaborate on this, but it is a subject I explore in great Bible-centric detail in my book *The God I Never Knew: How Real Friendship with the Holy Spirit Can Change Your Life.*)

After telling me that, yes, I was indeed destined to ultimately be a senior pastor, the Lord went on to let me know that this was something that would not happen right away for me. Indeed, He was very specific. He said I would become a senior pastor of a church when I was thirty-eight years old. In other words, in seven years.

At that point in my life, seven years into the future seemed like an eternity away. So I just tucked this nugget of direction away in my heart and made it a matter of prayer on those occasions when the Lord brought it to my remembrance.

The years that followed were filled with parenting, learning, and growing—both in my personal spiritual life and in my ministry experience. Olen
was a wonderful mentor, and I learned much about leading a congregation from
watching and listening to him.

Of course, as my thirty-eighth year approached, I couldn't help but wonder
what door the Lord would open to fulfill His yes to me all those years earlier. For
most of that time, my default assumption was that I would transition into leading Shady Grove Church whenever Olen decided he was ready to retire. But in
the final months of that seven-year period of preparation, I started to sense that
perhaps that was not what the Lord had in store for me.

Finally, on the day before my thirty-eighth birthday, the picture sharpened.
Something happened that made it clear to me that it might be several more years
before the senior pastor position at Shady Grove would be open. In hindsight,
this was clearly God's providential hand working for the good of everyone involved—Shady Grove included. But at that moment, it forced me to reexamine
my expectations and plans.

Immediately following this revelation, I was speaking with a few close
friends about the news. I wondered out loud if perhaps there might be another
existing church somewhere in America that needed a senior pastor. Then someone threw out the suggestion that I should simply plant a church in another part
of the Dallas-Fort Worth Metroplex.

Someone else jumped on the idea and pretty soon a what-if discussion was
underway. At first my response was, "Hey, that might be a good idea. I could
start the church far enough away from Shady Grove that it wouldn't tend to
draw members away…"

I was getting caught up in the hypothetical flow of the conversation when
suddenly a holy fear swept over me. I blurted out, "Wait! Stop! We can't be talking about this. I can't run down this road in my mind because God hasn't spoken to me about it."

The presumption of even considering a move of that magnitude without having a clear word from God made the hair on the back of my neck stand up. I said, "I love you guys and appreciate the support, but this simply isn't something we can talk about unless God speaks."

I took the next day to be alone with God and pray. I had a wonderful time of fellowship with the Lord, and in the process He directed me to two passages that pointed me in the direction of my God-ordained destiny.

The first was Genesis chapter 35. In this passage, the Lord spoke to Jacob and said, "Arise, go up to Bethel and dwell there; and make an altar there to God" (Genesis 35:1). As my eyes fell across this verse, the Holy Spirit strongly witnessed that it had special meaning for me in this moment. I recalled that *Bethel* (Beth-El) literally means "house of God."

God's instruction in this verse was quite literally, "Get up, move to another place, and build a place of worship—a house of God." For a preacher asking God what his next move is supposed be, this verse was packed with significance and meaning.

⮈ Keys to a Blessed Church

> When faced with a major decision or challenge, don't make a move without first getting alone with God and obtaining His counsel.
>
> Your word is a lamp to my feet and a light for my path. (Psalm 119:105, NIV)

Then the Lord found a way to direct my attention to another, even more obscure, passage—Deuteronomy 11. This entire chapter contains God's instructions to His people as they are about to move in and finally possess the land of promise. These verses are filled with references to taking a new land, and each one seemed to speak to me.

The next-to-last verse in the chapter rolled like thunder through my spirit:

> You are about to cross the Jordan to enter and take possession of the land
> the LORD your God is giving you. (Deuteronomy 11:31, NIV)

In the years since that day, God has used this rich chapter to speak to me on scores of occasions. (I'll share a few of these later on.) For now just know that I walked away from that day of prayer, study, and communing with my heavenly Father with a clear word about my future.

Planting a church wasn't merely a *good* idea; it was a *God* idea for me. I discussed this direction with Olen, and he responded with characteristic grace and wisdom. He recommended that we take what I had shared with him to the elders of Shady Grove, let them hear my heart, and get their take on how to proceed.

This could not have been an easy season for my friend and mentor. Olen was like a father to me and I like a son to him. Hearing of my planned direction was like a business owner's son suddenly declaring that he didn't want to take over the family business.

Ultimately, we all agreed that I should step away from Shady Grove before beginning any new endeavor. This would minimize any tendency for current Shady Grove members with a special affinity for me to try to follow me to my new work.

I was in complete agreement. I didn't want to launch this new phase of my life and ministry in the wrong way. The words of Deuteronomy 11 had made it clear to me that, if I wanted God's blessing on my time in this new land, I needed to enter it in absolute purity and obedience.

> Be careful, or you will be enticed to turn away and worship other gods
> and bow down to them. Then the LORD's anger will burn against you,
> and he will shut the heavens so that it will not rain and the ground will
> yield no produce, and you will soon perish from the good land the LORD
> is giving you. (Deuteronomy 11:16–17, NIV)

Next I asked Olen and the Shady Grove elders if they wanted to play a key role giving birth to this new work by officially planting my church and serving as its covering. After praying about it, the sense of the group was that Shady Grove was not to be the parent of this embryonic church. Once again, these men were hearing clearly from the Lord, as future events would bear out.

Throughout this season I had sought the counsel of Jimmy Evans, the pastor of Trinity Fellowship Church in Amarillo, Texas. Trinity was and is one of the finest, healthiest churches I've ever seen. Under Jimmy's leadership, the church has grown from about nine hundred members to more than eight thousand—this in a community with a population under two hundred thousand. He and his wife, Karen, are also the founders of a remarkable marriage and family ministry called MarriageToday.

In those years, Trinity Fellowship had organized and led a cooperative association of like-minded churches in West Texas, New Mexico, and Oklahoma. Trinity Fellowship Association of Churches (TFAC) had provided counsel, covering, ministry, and help to dozens of young churches in and around the Texas panhandle.

After hearing of Shady Grove's decision, I went to Jimmy for wise counsel. After praying about it, he came back to me with a suggestion that proved to be a heaven-sent solution.

He suggested I come on staff at TFAC for a season and preach as an evangelist at the various TFAC member churches as needed. This would provide a base of income for my family while I honored my commitment to Shady Grove to wait a season before starting another church. This I did with gratitude while pressing into God for specific direction about matters such as *where* to plant the church, *what* to call it, and *when* to begin.

A number of confirming signs had nudged us toward Southlake, Texas, a rapidly growing bedroom suburb of both Dallas and Fort Worth.

As for the name, the Lord used the Old Testament's Jacob once again to point the way. I was praying and reading the Word with this location question in mind when I came across the twenty-eighth chapter of Genesis. This is the passage in which Jacob famously slept out under the stars, so ill-equipped that he had to use a stone for a pillow. In a dream he saw heaven open up and angels rising and descending between heaven and earth.

In his dream, Jacob then had an encounter with God Himself in which God made a remarkable promise to him. Upon waking up, Jacob was understandably excited. He cried out,

> "Surely the LORD is in this place, and I wasn't even aware of it!" But he was also afraid and said, "What an awesome place this is! It is none other than the house of God, the very gateway to heaven!" (Genesis 28:16–17, NLT)

One phrase leapt out at me: "the very gateway to heaven." What Jacob described in his excitement that morning was exactly my heart's desire for this new church. I wanted it to be a place where people encountered the presence of God. Where people who had never experienced the love, power, and peace of God would feel it the moment they walked in the door and declare, "Surely the Lord is in this place."

Always an evangelist to my core, I wanted desperately to lead and steward a place that pointed people to the God who loves them by introducing them to the Way, Jesus Christ. In other words, to have this new place be a supernatural connecting point...a gateway.

So, Gateway Church it was.

God was equally vocal and specific about the timing of our launch. One day in the early months of 2000, I was reading a book that made reference to a church that had been launched on an Easter Sunday. This got me thinking about the pros and cons of beginning the church on that day. Part of me felt that no day could be more appropriate. After all, Resurrection Sunday is the day the Son of God conquered death and the grave, opening the way for all mankind to come to God and enter heaven. On the practical side, it's the day of the year people who are not deeply involved in a church are most likely to attend a service.

Still, I didn't want a *good* idea. I wanted *God's* idea. Throughout my adult life, God has used my wife, Debbie, to confirm His voice to me and impart wise perspective. So I laid my book aside and walked into the next room where Debbie was reading.

I said, "Honey, I think I may have gotten some direction from the Lord about when we're supposed to have the first service."

She looked up from her book and said, "I think I've just heard from God about that too."

"Really?" I said, trying not to look too hurt or disappointed that God wasn't speaking only and exclusively to me.

"Yes," she continued. "Easter Sunday." She had just been reading a book about a church that had experienced a major outpouring of God's presence during an Easter service.

"That's what I was thinking!" I said. "Let's call Jimmy Evans and see what he thinks."

When I got Jimmy on the phone, I excitedly told him that Debbie and I believed we'd heard from the Lord about exactly when to launch Gateway Church. Before I could drop the news flash, Jimmy said, "Oh, I know when you're supposed to launch. It's Easter."

As if that wasn't ample confirmation, not too many days later I was in a church service in which a wonderful minister and friend, Wayne Drain, was speaking. Now Wayne has a very sensitive heart to the voice of the Lord and is used often and mightily by God to deliver words of encouragement and comfort to others. In this service he was right in the middle of delivering such a message to a member of the congregation when he suddenly stopped, wheeled around, pointed at me and said these words: "Easter. Easter. Easter." Then he turned back around just as abruptly and continued his ministry message to that other person.

Needless to say, I felt I had clear direction from the Lord about when Gateway Church was to begin. It would be April 23, 2000. Easter Sunday. Whether there would be anyone in attendance besides me, Debbie, and our children was a separate question.

With the name, place, and timing of the launch established with clear words from heaven, I checked in once more with Olen and the elders at Shady Grove.

I let them know that TFAC was standing by with some seed funding to plant Gateway Church if I chose to use it, but that I wanted to make sure Shady Grove didn't want to do it themselves.

The response was gracious and supportive. They let me know that after praying about it they believed Trinity/TFAC was the ideal entity to play the role of midwife in this birth. They blessed us and let us know they were praying for us.

In the months leading up to that God-ordained Easter date, Debbie and I had the support and encouragement of Trinity Fellowship as well as that of some longtime friends from the area. We led a regular Bible study in our home that grew rapidly.

For our very first service, we took our seed money and rented a small ballroom in the Hilton hotel. It was far from the cheapest place in the area, but I wanted to honor the Lord by making our first service special. The fact was, we knew we didn't have the budget to meet there on an ongoing basis and we would need to find a much lower cost site going forward.

To our delight, we had one-hundred-eighty people in attendance. We were off to an amazing start.

3

Crazy Beginnings

I KNEW NOT TO GET TOO EXCITED about this large number the first week. Quite a few of those in attendance that first day were friends and well-wishers who were committed members of other churches. They came on that first Sunday simply to show their support and to bless us. I wasn't sure how many to expect on our second week.

After a frantic search for a more affordable alternative, we could only come up with a condemned, discount movie theater as an option. I suspected that a place that couldn't even make it as a dollar theater was not going to be a cosmetically pretty place—and my suspicions were confirmed. The floors were sticky with years of spilled soft drink accumulation. (As we would soon discover, so were many of the seats—people stuck to them.)

When Sunday rolled around again, we all arrived bright and early at the theater. Unfortunately, we couldn't get into the building. The building's maintenance man who was supposed to let us in (we hadn't been entrusted with a key) had gotten drunk the night before and overslept. Finally, in desperation, one bold member of our group went around to a back door and broke in.

To my disappointment, only sixty-eight people came to our second service. I went from exhilaration in week one to disappointment in week two. I have to confess that this was one of the darkest days of my life in ministry. Indeed, it was dark in more ways than one.

The theater in which we held the service had very poor lighting. To make matters worse, I was preaching on a black stage with a black velvet curtain as a backdrop. The topper on this disaster cake was my decision that day to wear black slacks, a dark shirt, and a black jacket.

After the service, one man told me that all he could see when I was preaching was a disembodied head and two hands waving around.

It wasn't the grand and glorious beginning I had envisioned—especially for an endeavor that I believed should exemplify excellence in every way. But it was a beginning. Still, it was obvious that we were going to have to find a more suitable location for our services. And quickly! We were two weeks old, and our growth curve was pointing in the wrong direction!

⇜ Keys to a Blessed Church

Don't succumb to discouragement when things begin smaller or more roughly than hoped. Pray for wisdom, obey the Lord's voice, and trust Him.

Do not despise these small beginnings, for the LORD rejoices to see the work begin. (Zechariah 4:10, NLT)

We prayed for wisdom, open doors, and divine connections. In gracious answer to our prayers, God put Pastor David Whitington in our path. He was and is the pastor of a great church in Southlake, Texas, called Christ Our King. Upon meeting with him, I asked if he had any interest in renting out his church building on Saturday evenings to a fledgling start-up. (Christ Our King only had services on Sunday morning at that time.)

David's response was wonderful. He said, "Absolutely! In fact, I've been praying for new churches to be started in Southlake. You're an answer to my prayers." David is one of the most kingdom-minded men I've ever met. His generous, secure spirit is too rare among pastors in the body of Christ.

Christ Our King's one hundred-fifty-seat sanctuary and classrooms gave us a suitable, reliable, easy-to-find location for a Saturday night service—one in which we could get established and begin to grow. And grow we did.

In that first year, typically I would preach on Saturday night, then after the service Debbie and I would go grab some dinner with another couple or two from among our new members. After the meal, Debbie, the kids, and I would head back to the church to clean the sanctuary and put everything in order for Christ Our King's services the next morning.

After fifteen months at Christ Our King Church, we moved to another rented facility—a former church location that was being used during the week as a preschool called A World of Learning. This location brought several advantages. We could squeeze up to three hundred people into the sanctuary; we could have multiple services on the weekend if needed; and, most importantly, we didn't have to set up and tear down for each service. We could invest in better sound, lighting, and projection equipment and leave it set up from week to week. This was huge.

Our move coincided with a surge of rapid growth that has actually never subsided. To get some perspective on this, consider the following: Before we moved in, another church had rented A World of Learning for several years while they built a permanent home. They were running about three hundred in attendance when they came and were about the same size when they moved out.

This church had chosen not to spend any money on improving or updating the rented facility. It's easy to understand their logic. After all, they didn't own the place and were focusing all their financial resources on building their permanent facility.

We hoped to buy land and build a building too, but we took a different approach. We immediately spent $75,000 updating a building we didn't own.

We started with a single Sunday morning service. After we outgrew it, we added another, quickly followed by a Saturday night service. Yet the rapid growth continued.

In fact, we moved into A World of Learning with about two hundred members and regular attendees. When we moved into a building of our own fifteen months later, we numbered more than two thousand and were running five services per weekend.

Please understand, it's not my intention to be boastful. It is just vital that you understand how very amazing this thing is that God has done before our eyes. It's important to document the size and scope of this miracle before I present to you the principles and precepts that made that miracle possible.

In other words, I need you to grasp the magnitude of the blessing before I tell you what I think made us bless-able.

During that fifteen-month period of extraordinary growth, we located thirteen acres of suitable land fronting the busy main commercial street running through Southlake. By God's grace and all of our members giving sacrificially, we paid cash for this land, $1.4 million! We then formulated what we thought was a financially prudent yet forward-thinking plan for our very first home of our own.

We would build a large shell of a structure but build out only half of it initially, leaving the other half as space for expansion as we grew further in the future. In fact, our architectural drawings involved a brilliant way to create a simple sanctuary at first, but when growth demanded it, to enable us to simply knock out a wall and more than double the available sanctuary space. The first phase of the plan created a fan-shaped seating arrangement—essentially a quarter-round allowing for about six hundred fifty seats. With the removal of the wall, phase two would create seating for sixteen hundred by expanding that fan-shaped design into a full half-circle.

It was a pretty clever approach. But we outsmarted ourselves. It took twenty-four months to get Phase 1 designed and built. By the time we were ready to move out of World of Learning and into our first true home, we had already outgrown it.

From day one, we had to start with three weekend services in the new location! And that meant we needed to begin Phase 2 planning and budgeting immediately. It took eight months to build out the empty half of our building and by the time it was ready, we were back to having five services with more than three thousand people attending each weekend.

It was an exciting day when we held our first service in the fully built-out sanctuary. Exciting for me, not only because it represented a major milestone in our journey with God and wonderful demonstration of His grace, but also a somewhat selfish reason: at least for a time we could go back to having only three services!

That schedule was short-lived, however. Over the next six years we would need to add a third, a fourth, a fifth, and ultimately a sixth service, while also adding multiple services at two satellite campuses and one at a nearby movie theater. (Yes, a movie theater! But this one was very new and nice. To my knowledge, nobody ever stuck to a seat.)

Obviously throughout these first amazing few years, I didn't ride this rocket alone. How Gateway came to be the ministry home for one of the most amazing teams of men and women I've ever seen is part of what I'll share in the chapters ahead. There were significant stretches of time in which we added a key pastor or ministry position per month. We frequently had months in which we added two or three.

In our tenth year of existence, we moved from that location into what is the current home of Gateway Church. A few years earlier, the Lord had led us to a hundred-eighty-acre parcel of prime real estate fronting a major highway, roughly a mile away from our existing location. It was (and still is) a beautiful piece of property, with trees, gently rolling hills, and several spring-fed ponds. In a later section I'll share some of the spiritual principles that guided us in the acquiring of this land. For now, just know that this process was as miraculous as the previous steps on our road.

Before we turned even a single spade of soil on that property, we invested in the creation of a long-term master plan for the new property. If we had learned anything during the previous years in the life of our church, it was that if you are hearing from God, you can't dream bigger than God can deliver. And on paper, the size of this dream was staggering.

Phase 1 would be a one-hundred-million dollar, four-thousand-seat sanctuary with support spaces for children's ministry and adult classrooms. On November 13, 2010, we held our first service in the new facility with exuberant worship born of deep gratitude to God for His great grace and unmerited blessing. Once again, our people had given sacrificially during one of the worst financial recessions of our lifetime.

As I mentioned at the outset, our growth continues. In fact, as I write these words, we're adding an additional Saturday evening service to our schedule, bringing us back to five per weekend at our main Southlake campus as well as four and five, respectively, in our two satellite locations. In the past twelve months, we've grown an additional 40 percent!

Now I know I have cited a lot of numerical evidence in describing Gateway's journey, but I don't want to give the wrong impression. The fact is, at its heart, ours is *not* a story of growth. It is a story of *health*.

We understand that our growth is a by-product of our health and God's blessing. Why? Because healthy things grow. And in the sections that follow, I'll share many of the keys and principles that I believe contribute to health, blessing, and growth.

These are not my insights alone. Far from it! What follows is the collective, accumulated wisdom and understanding of many people. Once again, this isn't my story. I just get to be the one who tells it. Let's get started.

 PART 2

Blessed Vision

4

It's Okay to Have
a Vision to Grow

THE YOUNG PASTOR ACROSS THE TABLE HAD SUDDENLY become apologetic. He had begun with an enthusiastic account of how God had called him to walk away from the security and familiarity of his position as a singles pastor at a large metropolitan church, step out into the unknown, and launch a church of his own halfway across the country.

I asked him what he thought God had shown him about what his church was called to do and be. In other words, I asked him about his *vision*. As he spoke, his eyes lit up with infectious enthusiasm and his pace of speaking accelerated.

After talking for a bit about mission, methods, and some of the ministries he envisioned launching from within the church, he started talking about numbers. He mentioned what kind of attendance and membership he saw his church having in three years, five years, and ten years into the future. But then midsentence, he began to sheepishly throw in disclaimers about how he knew that numbers weren't everything; that he would be content to take a small flock into deep waters if that's what the Lord wanted; and for good measure, he threw in the old cliché about only "counting people because people count."

He needn't have apologized. I understood his desire to impact large numbers of people and to the see the reach and influence of his ministry expand to great size. The fact is, it's okay to want to grow.

There is something God put in almost all of us that longs to see small things grow into big ones. It's been that way ever since God placed Adam and Eve in the Garden of Eden and commanded them, "Be fruitful and multiply; fill the earth" (Genesis 1:28). Jesus's parable of the talents is all about being rewarded for bringing kingdom increase to that with which we've been entrusted (see Matthew 25:14–30).

I've met thousands of entrepreneurs and business owners in my years in ministry. And in all that time I've never met one who, after choosing to endure all the hardship and labor and risk required to bootstrap a business, hoped that his business would stay small and insignificant. I've never talked to a farmer who—after buying seed on credit, toiling diligently day after day preparing the soil, planting, fertilizing, and irrigating—didn't pray that God would send all the rain and sun necessary to produce a bumper crop. Coaches want their teams to win. Architects want to see their buildings built and utilized. Writers want their books to be read by as many people as possible.

God made us to want to bring increase.

Given that truth, I'm not sure why we we're supposed to be shocked or offended when someone who is called and equipped to shepherd a flock has a desire to see that flock grow healthy and to multiply many, many times over. Nevertheless, we pastors are often made to feel that our dreams of broad reach and wide impact are somehow inappropriate.

There is nothing inherently ungodly or unseemly about wanting to impact very large numbers of people with the light and life of the gospel. Like pretty much every other aspect of the Christian life, it all comes down to the motivations and attitudes of our hearts. An evangelist can desire to fill a stadium because he has a burning passion to see lost people come to Jesus. But another may desire the very same thing because he is insecure and craves validation or affirmation. And a third can simply be striving to outdo a fellow evangelist out of a petty spirit of competitive pride. "For man looks at the outward appearance, but the LORD looks at the heart" (1 Samuel 16:7).

Nevertheless, when born of the right motives, there is nothing unnatural or unspiritual about growth and large impact being key elements of one's ministry vision.

Allow me to share something here that I have revealed to very few people over the last twenty years. Shortly after I had that initial conversation with Olen Griffing in which he planted the idea in my heart that I might one day be the senior pastor of a church—years before I ever launched Gateway—the Lord gave me a staggering vision for the church I would one day found.

⌒§ Keys to a Blessed Church

> It's okay to want to grow. It's part of the way God made us. But we must always monitor our motives and attitudes.
>
> > Neither do we go beyond our limits by boasting of
> > work done by others. Our hope is that, as your faith
> > continues to grow, our area of activity among you
> > will greatly expand. (2 Corinthians 10:15, NIV)

It came in a vivid dream one night—the kind you awaken from with complete recollection and a powerful awareness that it was no ordinary dream. In it, I was standing before the throne of God in heaven. Around me I could see a multitude of people too great to count. Then in the dream, the Lord spoke to me and said, *I want a church with thirty thousand people in one location.* He then spoke other specific things to me about having impact far beyond the walls of a single church. It's not necessary to share those additional aspects of my vision, but they did involve very large numbers—numbers that seemed far, far beyond the realm of possibility at the time. But the same was true of the thought of a thirty-thousand-member church in a single location. It just seemed crazy and unattainable.

Keep in mind, on the night of this dream I was just a young, raw associate pastor at a midsized church. The thought of that many people worshiping together in one location was more than I could wrap my little brain around. Seven years later when we launched Gateway Church with fewer than two hundred people, that thought should have seemed just as absurd. But it didn't to me. I had spent seven years nurturing a God-given vision.

Of course, I didn't brag or boast to others about this vision. I took a lesson from Joseph in Genesis, who got himself into trouble by spouting off carelessly and foolishly about his God-given visions of bigger things ahead. Instead I followed the example of Mary (the mother of Jesus) and just pondered and treasured God's amazing words in my heart (see Luke 2:19). I was very careful about whom I shared it with, which is a key aspect of *stewarding* the vision God has given you.

Now, as I write, almost twelve years have passed since Gateway's founding and, as you know by now, that vision doesn't seem far-fetched at all anymore. Indeed, if our past and current growth trends continue, we'll be knocking on the door of thirty thousand in the next year or two. Perhaps sooner. And we're seeing other aspects of that vision unfold before our eyes as well.

I have much more to share with you regarding receiving and sharing vision, but first there is an additional principle about growth that is important to understand.

5

Health-Growth Connection

HERE'S A DEEP, COSMIC TRUTH FOR YOU: HEALTHY THINGS GROW. God has woven this principle into the very fabric of creation. The converse of this is true as well. When a living thing becomes unhealthy, growth stops and even reverses. Ask any farmer or gardener. Or take a look at a vivid illustration of this in Jesus's parable of the soils:

> Behold, a sower went out to sow. And as he sowed, some seed fell by the wayside; and the birds came and devoured them. Some fell on stony places, where they did not have much earth; and they immediately sprang up because they had no depth of earth. But when the sun was up they were scorched, and because they had no root they withered away. And some fell among thorns, and the thorns sprang up and choked them. But others fell on good ground and yielded a crop: some a hundredfold, some sixty, some thirty. He who has ears to hear, let him hear! (Matthew 13:3–9)

Here Jesus is speaking metaphorically of the human heart and how the spiritual fruit-bearing nature of God's Word tends to either prosper or decline, depending upon the conditions of soil (heart) into which the seeds (the Word) fall. But Jesus has chosen this particular metaphor because it is universally understood that growth is connected to health.

Peter clearly had the health-growth connection in mind when he wrote, "As newborn babes, desire the pure milk of the word, *that you may grow thereby*"

(1 Peter 2:2). But what about the church? What about the kingdom Jesus came to establish and rule? In one of Isaiah's prophecies about the coming Messiah, we get an interesting bit of information. We often quote the first part of this at Christmastime:

> For unto us a Child is born,
> Unto us a Son is given;
> And the government will be upon His shoulder.
> And His name will be called
> Wonderful, Counselor, Mighty God,
> Everlasting Father, Prince of Peace.
> Of the increase of His government and peace
> There will be no end. (Isaiah 9:6–7)

Do you see it? The prophet Isaiah looked down through the halls of history and saw the promised Messiah taking the throne—"the government will be upon His shoulder." And he saw that the King's rule of peace would grow—and never stop growing!

Of course it keeps growing. Any kingdom ruled by Jesus would be healthy. And healthy things grow!

This means that if your vision involves *growth,* your real objective should be *health.* Whether a church, ministry, or organization is involved, you can be confident that if you pursue health, growth will be a naturally occurring by-product.

Not everyone does this, however. I've seen many pastors and business owners whose all-consuming focus was growth, growth, growth. Organizational health as a goal simply wasn't on their radar. And it is possible to grow rapidly without health…for a time. But ultimately—like the plants from seed that fell upon rocky soil in Jesus's parable—unhealthy growth proves unsustainable and ultimately collapses under its own weight. An organization that grows that way is the proverbial flash in the pan.

✑ Keys to a Blessed Church

Growth without real health is unsustainable. If you want growth, pursue and monitor health.

> He shall be like a tree
> Planted by the rivers of water,
> That brings forth its fruit in its season,
> Whose leaf also shall not wither;
> And whatever he does shall prosper. (Psalm 1:3)

So here's a bottom-line principle where health and growth are concerned: embrace growth but pursue health—knowing that health is the vital prerequisite, cause, and sustainer of growth. That's why much of the remainder of this book will focus on keys to cultivating a healthy, blessed church.

6

Predecessor of Vision

I'M A PREACHER, NOT A WRITER. MAYBE THAT'S WHY for much of my early life in ministry, I didn't care for Habakkuk 2:2. You, no doubt, are familiar with this verse. And it would be impossible to address the subject of receiving and imparting vision without referencing this passage:

> Then the LORD answered me and said: "Write the vision and make
> it plain on tablets, that he may run who reads it."

It's the classic, go-to verse on spiritual vision. Still, for quite a while I cringed every time I read it. Why? As I said, I'm a preacher, not a writer. I get great joy out of communicating spiritual truth verbally, but I'm not wired to enjoy the process of writing. I'm nothing like my amazing friend and mentor, Dr. Jack Hayford, who is as eloquent and inspiring on paper as he is on the platform. I recall once asking Jack what he did to relax. His answer was, "I write." I remember thinking, *You find that relaxing? I find it painful.* It was a little like discovering that your firefighter friend's primary hobby is putting out fires in his backyard. I just didn't get it.

So, you may be wondering how a guy like me who hates to write has written several books. Actually, I did it by *preaching* them. For each book, I taught the content live to a group of people. It was the only way I was ever going to get what was in my heart out there. Then I worked with a skilled writer who is a longtime member of my church—a man who knows my heart, my theology, and my voice—to transfer what I preached to the written page.

If putting what's in your heart down on paper comes easily to you, more power to you. But if you're like me, don't be too proud to ask for help! Of course, being able to write a God-given vision presumes that you have one. And I believe I know what precedes vision.

✎ Keys to a Blessed Church

> You can't communicate vision unless you have received vision from the Lord.
>
> > Now when they saw the boldness of Peter and John, and perceived that they were uneducated and untrained men, they marveled. And they realized that they had been with Jesus. (Acts 4:13)

Bill Hybels, my close friend, a great man of God, and the senior pastor of the hugely influential Willow Creek Community Church, pointed me to the following important insight. To share it, I need to direct you to the story of Moses:

> Now it came to pass in those days, when Moses was grown, that he went out to his brethren and looked at their burdens. And he saw an Egyptian beating a Hebrew, one of his brethren. So he looked this way and that way, and when he saw no one, he killed the Egyptian and hid him in the sand. (Exodus 2:11–12)

Have you ever seen someone being severely beaten? I'm not talking about seeing violence on television or YouTube, but right before your own eyes. I hope not, because it's a horrible thing to see and hear.

I was a wild, rebellious kid and saw far too many fights growing up. I also participated in too many. As a result, I have very bad memories of fighting as a young man—especially because I lost most of the time. You see, I had a big mouth and little muscles. One particular bad memory I have is of a fight in which I received the worst beating I ever got in my life. It was five against two. Those were the toughest two guys I'd ever met. (Okay, that's a joke!)

My point is that it's upsetting to see someone being beaten. And that's what Moses saw that day. But Moses didn't just intervene in the fight. His passion and his indignation about what he saw were so great that he killed the Egyptian abuser. Murdered him!

Here's my point: what stirred Moses to action was an injustice that frustrated him. He saw something going on that he simply couldn't allow to continue any longer. He was compelled by frustration and inward passion to *do* something about it.

The next chapter in Exodus moves us forty years forward in Moses's life. While Moses had been around forty years of age when he killed the Egyptian taskmaster, in chapter 3 he's roughly eighty.

And the LORD said: "I have surely seen the oppression of My people who are in Egypt, and have heard their cry because of their taskmasters, for I know their sorrows." (Exodus 3:7)

Here God is basically saying, "I've seen. I know." In other words, "Moses, I've seen what you saw. What frustrates you frustrates Me."

This may strike you as odd or unorthodox to hear it phrased this way, but I believe *frustration* is a major precursor and indicator of vision. If you're not sure what God has ordained your ministry to do and be, perhaps you should begin by asking yourself, *What frustrates me?* If you are a current or prospective pastor, take some time in your quiet time and ask the Holy Spirit to make you mindful of what other churches do that frustrates you. I believe the answers will begin to illuminate and clarify your specific vision for a church.

7

When You "Can't Stands No More"

Vision can come from what Bill Hybels calls "holy discontent." (In fact, Bill has written a wonderful book with that term as the title.) Vision can spring from your perception of an injustice that motivates you to action. Because you have been redeemed and have a pastor's heart, it is very possible that whatever is frustrating you is also frustrating God.

If you are of a certain age, you probably remember Saturday morning cartoons. Before there were dedicated cable channels showing nothing but cartoons 24/7—before there were cable channels *at all*—a kid had to wait until Saturday morning to watch cartoons. It's difficult for my children to comprehend this, but you may remember when there were only three or four channels. And in our house, I was the remote control. "Turn it to channel 4, Robert. *The Ed Sullivan Show* is about to start."

In *Holy Discontent*, Hybels illustrates this important concept by pointing back to an old cartoon series. Perhaps you remember the *Popeye* cartoons. Olive Oyl was our hero's girlfriend, and his archenemy was Bluto.

What would happen in every show? Bluto would commit some injustice or outrage. Popeye would endure it for a time, but eventually he would get fed up. When he just couldn't take it anymore, he would say, "That's all I can stands, and I can't stands no more." The pronouncement would always be followed by spinach eating, supernatural strength impartation, and mopping up the floor with Bluto.

Here's my question for you: What is it you "can't stands no more"? Righting that wrong is a key to your vision for ministry.

It may be that for your whole life in ministry you've been seeing some things that bug you. You probably have observed a lot of good things too, but I suspect those things that cut against the grain of your convictions and passions are the ones that really stand out. There may be some things in other churches or ministries that aren't necessarily wrong...they're just wrong *for you*. It's just not the way that God has created you to do it.

As I mentioned previously, I attended and served at Shady Grove Church as an under-shepherd for sixteen years. Fourteen of those years were great. Pure ministry bliss. During those final two years, I was increasingly miserable. The church wasn't doing anything different. And they certainly weren't doing anything wrong. But in those final two years, my personal vision for ministry began to crystallize. As a direct result, I started seeing things that I couldn't "stands no more."

Again, it's not that these things were wrong; it's just there was something within me that envisioned something different. What Shady Grove was doing was perfectly consistent with the heart and vision of Pastor Olen Griffing. The fact is, Shady Grove was one of the churches God used to pioneer the worship revival that swept the globe several decades ago. That was in large part because Olen saw lifeless, rote worship being the norm in church, and it frustrated him. He endured services that lacked the presence of God—until he could "stands no more."

In those final two years at Shady Grove, as God began preparing my heart, I grew itchy to do some things a different way. But that didn't mean that I was rebellious. I was just finally ready to step into God's vision for me. I was experiencing a principle of stewardship Jesus revealed in His parable of the unwise steward:

And if you have not been faithful in what is another man's, who will give you what is your own? (Luke 16:12)

There is an obvious flip side of this spiritual principle: if you *have* been faithful with what is another man's, you may eventually be entrusted with what is your own. I believe I had been faithful with another man's God-given vision. As a result of that stewardship, I was about to be entrusted with a vision of my own. And when that vision began to take shape, it began stoking a fire of holy discontentment in me.

✌ Keys to a Blessed Church

What spiritual injustice bothers you most? Righting that wrong is a key to your vision for ministry.

> I was mute with silence,
> I held my peace even from good;
> And my sorrow was stirred up.
> My heart was hot within me;
> While I was musing, the fire burned.
> Then I spoke with my tongue. (Psalm 39:2–3)

As Gateway launched and began to grow, I learned more about what I couldn't "stands," and these frustrations helped inform and define the ultimate vision of the church.

For example, I learned quickly after launching the church that I couldn't bear the thought of not equipping people for ministry. I couldn't stand it. I wasn't going to have a church in which the work of ministry is done solely from the platform and by the paid ministers on staff. I couldn't stand the idea of being a church in which the members are spectators who merely outsource evangelism, outreach, and love of the hurting to others through their financial giving. As a ministry staff, we had to view our primary jobs as equipping the membership for ministry.

In a similar way, I couldn't stand the idea of doing church apart from consistently taking people into deeper levels of intimacy with God. One of the many things I loved about the vision and culture at Shady Grove was the value placed upon experiencing God's presence both corporately as a church body and individually. I knew we had to have that at Gateway Church but in a way suited to our unique calling and destiny.

I learned just how important this element was to my vision after I briefly departed from this value. There was a short season in the early days of the church in which I bought into the idea that we needed to dial back the intensity of our worship and experience of the Holy Spirit's activity in our services in order to be more "accessible" to unbelievers. It didn't last long. I couldn't "stands" it.

It has also become clear to me that the whole premise of the experiment was flawed. Why? Unbelievers are actually attracted to, not repelled by, the power and presence of God. Spiritually hungry seekers are looking for something authentic and transformative—something bigger than themselves.

Indeed, a significant portion of Gateway's astonishing growth over the years has been driven by people seeking a more meaningful encounter with God than they were having at their previous churches. In fact, at one point I actually asked to meet with another local pastor because I became alarmed at the number of his congregants who were now coming to Gateway. After speaking to enough of these new arrivals to discern a pattern, I called him up and said, "Can I meet with you?"

He agreed, and when we connected, after a bit of getting-to-know-you chatting, I got to the point: "I'm sure you know that quite a few people in your church are attending Gateway now."

He nodded.

"Well, I've noticed it too, and I want you to know I'm concerned about it. That's why I was compelled to ask for this meeting, even though it's an awkward and difficult conversation to have. In fact, the easiest thing in the world for me to do would be to remain silent while a steady stream of new members comes our way from your church. But the fact is, we're playing for the same team. We're not competitors; we're teammates, each with a specific role to play in the Coach's game plan. I want you to grow. I want your church to thrive and be all God wants it to be."

I think he could tell that I was utterly sincere, so at this point I had his undivided attention. Then I pressed on: "I think you have a hole in your vision for ministry. I say that because of what I'm hearing when I talk to your members. Would you mind sharing your vision for your church with me? I'd like to test my theory."

He said, "Sure," and then he proceeded to outline what was clearly a well-thought-out approach to minister to various groups through initiatives designed to serve the community. There was absolutely nothing wrong or unbiblical about anything he described. On the contrary, it was all great. But there was one thing I was listening for that I did not hear. There was nothing in his vision about providing people the opportunity to have regular, corporate encounters with the presence of God. There was a hole in his vision.

I recognized it only because I had suffered from the same kind of hole for a six-month period in our church's life (the period I just described)—all because I'd bought into the conventional wisdom of the time about being seeker sensitive.

I shared with him what I believed was the hole in his vision. His plan needed to change—to include a way for mature believers to continue to grow and deepen their relationship with Jesus. This pastor listened graciously and seemed to be receptive, but in the end, I'm not sure he embraced what I was trying to share with him.

8

The Core of My Early Church Vision

GOD PLANTS A WIDE VARIETY OF VISIONS in pastors' hearts because the world is a diverse place, and He wants to reach everyone, everywhere, with His saving love. Nevertheless, certain core elements should characterize every pastor and church; they are essential to what pastors and churches are called to do and be.

One at the top of that list is Jesus's final personal command to Peter: "Feed My sheep" (John 21:17). Sheep feeding will be a nonoptional, nonnegotiable element in every vision God gives to pastors. Why? Because that's what shepherds do. There was a lot I didn't understand when I launched Gateway Church, but I understood that. I knew the core of my calling as a pastor was to feed the sheep.

Without a doubt, my vision for Gateway Church crystallized, expanded, and deepened over the years, but from the very beginning there were three key things I was determined that, with God's grace and supernatural empowerment, we would do as a church. The following were the central goals of my vision:

1. We would deliver the most outstanding sermons you've ever heard.
2. We would provide the most extraordinarily skilled and Spirit-infused worship experience in which you've ever participated.
3. We would offer the best children's ministry your kids have ever experienced.

I know these vision goals sound arrogant. But that's the nature of God-given vision. When you let the Holy Spirit paint dreams and a vision upon the canvas of your heart, a picture will emerge that will stagger your imagination and test your faith. If the vision doesn't seem impossible to accomplish with your natural ability, it's probably not from God.

Throughout Scripture, whenever men and women of God received vision from Him and began to walk in it, they invariably had people pointing at them, asking, "Just who do you think you are?" We saw it happen with Joseph, Moses, Joshua, Caleb, David, and most of the prophets. Of course, Jesus got that more often than any of them:

> But the Pharisees and teachers of religious law said to themselves,
> "Who does he think he is? That's blasphemy! Only God can forgive
> sins!" (Luke 5:21, NLT)

The three core elements of my vision certainly would have seemed absurdly ambitious to any observer, but everyone involved understood that this vision was the promise under which Gateway Church was launched. I just decided that I would preach the best sermons that I could possibly preach, that we would have the best worship we could possibly have, and that we would have the best children's ministry we could possibly provide. God exceeded our expectations. That's what vision works in our lives and in the body of Christ.

⤚ Keys to a Blessed Church

> When you let the Holy Spirit paint a vision upon the canvas of your heart, a picture will emerge that will stagger your imagination and test your faith. If the vision doesn't seem impossible to accomplish with your natural ability, it's probably not from God.
>
> > But Moses said to God, "Who am I that I should go to Pharaoh, and that I should bring the children of Israel out of Egypt?" (Exodus 3:11)

We pursued excellence in each area of my vision. We prayed for help and supernatural empowerment in each of these areas. And we worked our tails off to get better in each of these areas.

I believe the Lord has honored those efforts and prayers. Over the years the second-most consistent comment we've received from new members is this: "We are here because of our kids. We visited once, and then they kept asking when we were going to get to go back to the 'fun church.'"

So, what is the number one comment we've heard? It is this: "I didn't know I wasn't being fed until I came here." Again, that may sound prideful to ears that don't understand my heart. The fact is, anyone called to pastor can be an excellent sheep feeder. It doesn't require brilliance or talent. It requires only a hard-headed determination to prioritize your personal time with God, in His Word, and then to faithfully carry to your people what you receive in those times of fellowship and study.

By the way, feeding sheep well is the key to evangelism. Too many people assume that evangelism is the job of the pastor and church staff. Many pastors seem to think this way as well. But the key to winning our cities consists of healthy, well-fed sheep. Those are the kinds of sheep that reproduce out there in the workplace, the marketplace, and the neighborhood. Our job is to train up everyday evangelists and send them out, filled with the Word and the influencing power that comes from having been in God's presence.

9

Articulating the Vision

OKAY, SO YOU'VE GOT A VISION FROM GOD for your church and you've embraced the principle of the health-growth connection. Great.

It's one thing to receive vision from God. It's another thing to exercise good stewardship of that vision (more on that later). And still another thing to know how to properly articulate that vision to others.

To be honest, this third element did not come naturally to me. I've been called a man of vision, and I suppose it's true, if by it you mean developing the habit of taking the time to hear what God is saying. When God shows you things—what He wants to do in you, through you, and through others—it's not hard to have a God-given vision. But it has not always been easy for me to communicate that vision to others. This was especially true in the early years of launching the church.

In the early days I assumed everyone involved knew *why* we were starting a church. You start a church because the world needs churches. Right? Jesus is the answer to every need and every question. And as the body of Christ, the church is the physical presence of Jesus in the earth today. I sort of just figured that my vision for our church was to *be* the church, and then I assumed that if we just built it, everything else would take care of itself. And I assumed everyone around me saw it that way too.

Of course, "build the church" is not a vision. It's a broad-brushed, general exhortation. Build what kind of church? A church involved in what kinds of outreach? Reaching what types of people? Investing in what kinds of initiatives? Equipping the membership to do...what, specifically?

Not surprisingly, I got a lot of questions about vision from my leadership and staff in the first several years of our existence. In fact, at least once every three or four months during our first few years, I would be in a meeting with our elders and hear this statement: "We need to define the vision of the church."

My usual response was a flustered, stammering repetition of what I'd said before. "Well...uh, you know...my vision is to build this church...reach people... grow." That was usually followed by an awkward silence, and then we'd move on to the next topic—until the same issue came up again a few months later.

I can be a little slow sometimes, but it eventually became clear to me that, as a leader, shepherd, and Chief Visionary Officer (CVO), I was failing to fill a very specific, very real need of the elders and staff of Gateway Church. And the truth was, I had much more vision in my heart than I was expressing. The problem was that articulating it did not come naturally to me. I asked the Lord for help. And help arrived in the form of Tom Lane.

Tom was sent by heaven to be my Number Two, or in our parlance, our executive senior pastor. He had served in this very role for Jimmy Evans at Trinity Fellowship Church in Amarillo, Texas, for years and is uniquely gifted for it. One of his many gifts is his ability to handle much of the administrative detail of running the church, leaving the senior pastor free to focus on that which is most vital for the success of the endeavor—spending time with God and in His Word, hearing from heaven, and preparing to feed the sheep (see John 21:17).

Gateway Church was about three years old when God began to simultaneously move on all of our hearts (mine, Tom's, and most importantly, Jimmy Evans's) about Tom's transitioning from working alongside Jimmy in Amarillo and joining us at Gateway. Within six months, Tom and his wonderful wife, Jan, were in place at our church.

Of course, Tom was no stranger to me and Gateway Church, nor we to him. As you'll recall, Trinity Fellowship and its church network had planted Gateway in the very beginning—providing a salary for me and another staff member in those preparatory months and providing the seed money that launched us and kept us going until we got our feet under us. Thus, releasing

Tom Lane to come and join the work at Gateway wasn't the first gracious gift Jimmy and Trinity Church had given to us. But it was the greatest one. It was massively sacrificial.

One of the first things Tom did in getting settled into his position at Gateway was ask me if we had a written document describing the vision God had given me for the church. (That vision thing again!) I did my flustered stammering thing once more in response and ultimately handed him a random collection of legal-pad notes, journal entries, and other scraps of paper I'd accumulated over the years.

From these, it was evident to Tom that I did indeed have a clear, compelling, God-given vision for Gateway. It was equally clear to him that I needed help in getting what God had put in my heart into a form that could provide direction to others. Tom then immediately went to work to provide that help. A little later in this section, I'll share in detail the written vision that emerged, but for now I'll summarize it this way: When I was saying "build the church," I wasn't calling for growth for growth's sake or size for size's sake. My vision was not to merely *gather people* but to *make disciples.*

Tom began the process by getting a handle—in general, theoretical, and spiritual terms—on what I believed the Lord had told me that Gateway Church was to be. With pen and paper in hand, he would ask me very specific questions to gauge how the elements of that vision might translate into specific programs, priorities, and practices.

Tom: Do you see the church offering special ministry to single people?
Me: Yes!

Tom: Do you foresee having satellite campuses at some point in the future?
Me: Yes!

Tom: Do you foresee adding a traditional Sunday school to help new believers learn the Bible?

Me: No. But I see having an ongoing series of classes—perhaps on
       Wednesday nights—that focus on Bible books and biblical topics.
       These could provide members of our staff and membership who
       have a strong teaching gift a place to serve and utilize their gifting
       while advancing our mission to make disciples.

Tom: Do you foresee the church having a K–12 Christian school at some
       point?

Me: Yes, but probably not for some time. That's a big undertaking.

And so this dialogue continued until Tom was able to produce a document
that clearly and accurately articulated in practical detail what I believed the Lord
had given me in spiritual theory.

Of course, the prerequisite to all that was having actually received that kind
of insight and direction from God. You can't communicate vision unless you
have received vision. Let me share a few keys to doing that in your own life and
ministry.

10

Writing the Vision

IF YOU'RE A TYPICAL PASTOR, YOU HAVE SHELVES SAGGING from the weight of books on leadership. There's a lot of great stuff out there—from pastors like John Maxwell and Bill Hybels, as well as those from business gurus like Jim Collins and Stephen Covey. It's all worthwhile. Of course, if you've read much of this kind of material at all, the importance of a clear vision and mission statement has been burned into your awareness.

Vision is indeed the most important weapon in a leader's arsenal. And as we've seen, a well-written vision statement is a key tool for helping everyone involved to know "what's important around here." As Habakkuk was told (and I'm paraphrasing here), "Write the vision and make it clear so that those who read it can run—and run in the right direction" (see 2:2).

Many pastors turn the crafting of the written vision over to the broader leadership team. The conventional wisdom is that you're more likely to get the whole team to buy into the vision if they're allowed a role in framing it. I think pastors need to be careful in this regard. It's very easy to have your vision diluted, corrupted, or hijacked by the well-meaning ideas of others. While there can certainly be value in getting help in expressing what God has given you, it's vital to remember that vision starts with one person.

Survey Scripture; you don't find God imparting vision to a committee. He invariably spoke to one person. But note: He always expected that same one person to communicate the vision clearly to others. Why? Because vision can only be *accomplished* by a team. David had his mighty men. Moses had Aaron, Miriam, Joshua, and seventy elders. Jesus had His disciples.

Vision statements, mission statements, and statements of purpose often result from productive collaborative meetings. But in my experience, most people
will not remember them after the vision-purpose-mission retreat is over. And a
year later, you're likely to hear a conversation in the hall that goes something like
this:

> Staff Member A: We should do the XYX initiative. After all, our mission
> statement says, "Blah, blah, blah..."
> Staff Member B: Wait. I thought that was our purpose statement.
> Staff Member C: No, that's in our vision statement, or is it...?

Yes, you must write the vision so those who read it can run in the right direction. And if you are so led, by all means get your staff and leadership involved
in extending that vision into the crafting of mission and purpose statements. But
let me encourage you to make sure that what emerges is something people can
understand, remember, and grab hold of.

The best church mission statement I've ever heard is the one employed by
Bill Hybel's Willow Creek Community Church: "Turning irreligious people
into fully devoted followers of Christ." I wish I had thought of that. Simple.
Relatable. Actionable. Defining.

Vision, mission, and purpose documents serve an important purpose—and
toward the end of this chapter, I'll share some of Gateway's with you. But none
of these, which are all created for an internal audience, should be confused
with a church slogan or positioning statement, which is created for an external
audience—the community around you. Such a slogan is less about leadership
and more about marketing. (For the record, God is not opposed to sound marketing and advertising; it's just that they can never take the place of anointing,
evangelism, and outreach.)

Early in Gateway's life as a church, I asked the Lord to provide a positioning
statement that would accurately and attractively present our heart to the community. In response He gave me a simple expression of His heart: *We're all about
people.* It remains our positioning statement to this day.

ᴥᶂ Keys to a Blessed Church

> Vision is the most important weapon in a leader's arsenal.
> And as we've seen, a well-written vision statement or docu-
> ment is a key tool for helping everyone involved to know
> what is essential to your ministry.
>
> Where there is no revelation, the people cast off
> restraint. (Proverbs 29:18)

Over the years, some have questioned the wisdom of that statement. "How can you say that you're all about people?" they ask. "Shouldn't you be all about Jesus?"

Of course, enjoying relationship with God through His Son, Jesus Christ, is at the heart of all we are. But we recognize that we are the body of Christ on the earth. We are His representatives to a lost and dying world. It's a world Jesus gave His life to save. We boldly and confidently proclaim that we're all about people because we're worshiping and serving and representing the One who so loved the world that He gave His only Son. Since we are all about God, we are all about what He is all about: people!

So what is Gateway Church's vision statement? Over the years a short, seven-element sentence has emerged; I believe that it accurately expresses the vision God gave me. If you were to stop any member of our pastoral staff and ask that person about the vision of Gateway Church, you will almost certainly hear the following reply:

> The vision of Gateway Church is to see people saved, healed, set free,
> discipled, equipped, empowered, and serving in ministry.

I could expand upon any and all of these seven outcomes at great length and show you how they translate into priorities and ministries. But that simple sentence is my vision in a nutshell. It's what I meant in those early days when I was saying, "Just build the church." It's what God planted in my heart all those years ago, only now it's been articulated in a clear, concise, contagious sentence. It's the compass by which we steer our spending. It's the yardstick by which we measure our progress. It's the standard by which we evaluate new programs and proposed initiatives.

From that has come a mission statement that outlines what we want to help every church member experience. Our mission is to activate people in spiritual formation in four areas (we call them the Four Bs):

1. Believing in Jesus
2. Belonging to His Family
3. Becoming His Disciple
4. Building His Kingdom

A well-articulated vision should describe more than what you intend to do. It will ideally express *how* you intend to conduct yourself. After all, before you can *do* something, you have to *be* something. Being precedes doing. In other words, you have to answer the question, What values and virtues must characterize our community and culture if we're going to faithfully carry out this vision? To that end, we established twelve, Word-based guiding principles to serve as goals and guides for our actions as staff and as a church body:

1. Unity (see Psalm 133)
2. Excellence (see Matthew 5:16)
3. Humility (see James 4:6)
4. Service (see Ezekiel 44; Matthew 20:28)
5. Faith (see Hebrews 11:6)
6. Equity (see Jeremiah 22:13–16, James 2:1–4)
7. Compassion (see 1 Peter 3:8)
8. Submission (see Romans 13:1)
9. Integrity (see Philippians 2:15)
10. Generosity (see 2 Corinthians 9:6)
11. Kingdom Centered (see 1 Corinthians 12:14–27)
12. Truth-and-Spirit Centered (see John 1; 14; 16)

A vision God can bless is a vision you allow Him to give you. It will require both great faith and a holy audacity to receive it. You may need to first identify your holy discontentment in order to understand the vision. But eventually, you're going to have to find a way to communicate it to others in clear, compelling ways if you're going to see it come to life.

 PART 3

Blessed Shepherds

11

Leading Is Not an Option

I USED TO THINK, WHY WOULD ANYONE IN THE WORLD FOLLOW ME? Many struggling pastors over the years have admitted to suffering similar doubts. "I love to preach and teach," they tell me. "I love to serve and share. But I don't consider myself a natural leader."

I understand. But the fact remains, if you are called to pastor, you are called to lead. It's a key element in the job description. Still, we all tend to be overwhelmingly aware of our own flaws, failings, and weaknesses—our humanness. It doesn't help that people often put us on a spiritual pedestal. Rank-and-file church members, as well as people on the street, assume we pastors have a special 24/7 phone line to heaven and VIP passes to the throne of God that regular folks don't get. If only that were true!

The fact is, the ground is quite level at the foot of the Cross.

Whenever I'm tempted to actually buy into such a myth myself, I remember a funny story about the late David Wilkerson, the legendary pastor of Times Square Church in New York City. Two of David's four children and several of his grandchildren are members of Gateway Church, so it was my privilege to provide some ministry to the family after his sudden passing due to a car accident in April 2011.

At the funeral service, one of his kids shared about a season in Wilkerson's life—when he was in his seventies—of intensive prayer and Bible study. Apparently the subject of God's glory fascinated him. For about three months Wilkerson hid himself away in order to devote himself to passages of the Bible in which the glory of God had manifested itself. Wilkerson's desire and prayer was that he would grow so close to God—that he would be so full of God's presence and love—that it would literally be visible to others.

This wasn't a prideful thing. He was just an evangelist through and through, and evangelists can't help but desire to be walking, visible advertisements for God. In fact, at the beginning of this quest he told his wife, "I believe that I can get so close to God that people will see the *Shekinah* on my face, like Moses. That's what I'm praying for. I want people to walk up and ask me about Jesus, and then I can lead them to Him."

In any event, at the end of this intensive, three-month period of retreat and fellowship with God, David emerged and took his wife out to dinner at a restaurant. Throughout their meal, David noticed that one of the waitresses was frequently looking at him from across the room. He became increasingly certain that the young woman was staring at him. Finally, with obvious excitement, he mentioned it to his wife. "Gwen, that waitress over there sees the glory of God on my face. I just know it. She's perceiving that I've been with God!"

Sure enough, a few minutes later the waitress timidly approached the table. David sat up straight, cleared his throat, and mentally prepared to share a deeply spiritual answer to whatever question the woman had on her heart.

Finally she spoke and he heard her say, "I am so sorry, but I have been watching you since you came in and I just have to ask you…"

Here it comes, David thought.

"Are you Hugh Hefner?"

David was eventually able to laugh about the incident, but only after the initial shock and sting of disappointment wore off. It was bad enough that no one had noticed him spiritually glowing due to his close proximity to God. Even worse, the one person who had seemed to take notice of him mistook him for America's king of smut!

"Okay, I'm just human after all" was his conclusion.

The fact is, we're all mere mortals. And yet success in your role as pastor (or parent or business owner, for that matter) demands the ability to lead. And to raise up leaders around you.

ᴥᲫ Keys to a Blessed Church

> If you are called to pastor, you are called to lead. Still, we all tend to be overwhelmingly aware of our own flaws, failings, and weaknesses—our humanness. The fact is, the ground is quite level at the foot of the Cross.
>
> > "Who am I, O Lord GOD? And what is my house,
> > that You have brought me this far?" (2 Samuel 7:18)

In fact, for long-term success and health, that latter task, raising up leaders, is probably more vital than the former. Pastors—even those who are excellent leaders and efficient managers—will ultimately collapse under the demands of ministry and the stresses of growth if they don't learn the art and science of identifying, cultivating, and empowering new leaders around them.

In the chapters that follow, I'll share some of the spiritual and practical leadership keys I've discovered over the years—keys that are especially helpful for mere mortals like you and me who have been called to the office of shepherd.

12

To Feed and Lead

THE TWENTY-FIRST CHAPTER OF JOHN HAS BECOME a defining and life-anchoring passage for me as a pastor. The chapter records a remarkable conversation between the resurrected Jesus and the post-triple-denial Simon Peter. (Three times Peter denied even knowing his friend and mentor on the darkest night of Jesus's life.) Yet I have studied and meditated on this passage so often that I feel as if I were the one who took a walk with Jesus at the lakeshore that day.

The familiar passage merits citing at length:

So when they had eaten breakfast, Jesus said to Simon Peter, "Simon, son of Jonah, do you love Me more than these?"

He said to Him, "Yes, Lord; You know that I love You."

He said to him, "Feed My lambs."

He said to him again a second time, "Simon, son of Jonah, do you love Me?"

He said to Him, "Yes, Lord; You know that I love You."

He said to him, "Tend My sheep."

He said to him the third time, "Simon, son of Jonah, do you love Me?" Peter was grieved because He said to him the third time, "Do you love Me?"

And he said to Him, "Lord, You know all things; You know that I love You."

Jesus said to him, "Feed My sheep.

Most assuredly, I say to you, when you were younger, you girded yourself and walked where you wished; but when you are old, you will stretch out your hands, and another will gird you and carry you where you do not wish." This He spoke, signifying by what death he would glorify God. And when He had spoken this, He said to him, "Follow Me." (John 21:15–19)

In the original Greek there is an amazing amount of nuance and significance in the words exchanged between Jesus and Peter—meaning that does not come through in many of our English translations.

For example, when Jesus asked Peter, "Do you love me?" He used the Greek word *agape*—meaning the sacrificial, giving kind of love that God displays. But the first several times Peter replied, "Yes, Lord; You know that I love You," he used instead the word *phileo,* which connotes affection, friendship, trust, and devotion, but it is not the same as *agape.*

Peter wasn't being unkind or coy here. You have to remember that just days previous to this moment he had shot his mouth off to Jesus about sticking with Him to the bitter end, no matter what. And within twenty-four hours of making that declaration, Peter had denied Jesus three times. We can assume that in the devastating, guilt-racked hours after Jesus's crucifixion Peter had made a fierce inner vow to never boast like that again.

Never again will I allow my mouth to write checks my heart cannot cash, Peter must have sworn to himself. Then at the lakeshore Peter finds himself being asked by his risen Lord if he loves Him with the God kind of love. Peter's responses to Jesus's repeated question seem to indicate a powerful desire to avoid overpromising and underdelivering.

Notice also that after the first question-and-answer round, Jesus's response was, "Feed my lambs." "Lambs" is the correct English translation in this instance. The Greeks used a different word to refer to adult sheep. In fact, that's the word Jesus used in Round 2:

He said to him again a second time, "Simon, son of Jonah, do you love [agape] Me?"

He said to Him, "Yes, Lord; You know that I love [phileo] You."

He said to him, "Tend My sheep." (verse 16)

The Greek word translated "tend" is *poimainō,* and it connotes more than just feeding. It suggests nurturing, protecting, watching over—in other words, shepherding!

In Round 1 Jesus said, "Feed my lambs." In Round 2 He said, "Tend my sheep." And in Round 3? Jesus adjusts His exhortation once more:

He said to him the third time…, "Feed My sheep." (verse 17)

Of course, as we've already seen, Jesus didn't stop there. He went on to prophesy to Peter about His death.

Believe it or not, Jesus actually told Peter this to reassure him. Peter's responses in the conversation up to this point make it clear that Peter was not secure in his ability to stick to his commitments under pressure or persecution. What Peter didn't know at this point was that after His resurrection, Jesus would be sending the Holy Spirit to indwell and empower Peter. He couldn't possibly have imagined what a game changer the empowering, transforming presence of the Spirit would be in his ability to carry out the plans and purposes of God.

Jesus prophesied that a day would come when Peter needed to give his very life for Jesus—and that on that day he would stand strong! Jesus was essentially telling his friend, "Peter, you're going to die for Me." That had to have been the best bad news Peter ever received.

Put another way, Jesus was saying, "Being a shepherd is going to cost you your life." That's how serious this calling is. That's how seriously I've learned to take it. Today, if you cut me, I bleed sheep. Why? Because I am a shepherd. My most fundamental impulse is to protect the sheep. As a result, I will not allow anyone in my pulpit to beat the sheep. No one. Those who share the pulpit at

Gateway Church are sheep feeders. They are sheep encouragers. Sheep equippers. You get access to the sheep under my care only if you have a shepherd's heart and if you're willing to lay down your life for the sheep.

✌ Keys to a Blessed Church

It shocks most busy pastors to learn that I put more time into *feeding* than I do into *leading* (administrating).

So guard yourselves and God's people. Feed and shepherd God's flock—his church, purchased with his own blood—over which the Holy Spirit has appointed you as elders. (Acts 20:28, NLT)

In Jesus's three rounds of questioning, He laid out the spectrum of spiritual growth levels that a pastor-shepherd must address.

First: "Feed My lambs." In other words, feed the young ones, the new Christians, and the ones who are on their way to becoming believers. When you preach a sermon, make sure that the lambs get it too.

Second: "Tend My sheep." Get the flock—the church body as a whole—moving in the way they should go. Correct them. Raise a standard. "Convince, rebuke, exhort, with all longsuffering and teaching" (2 Timothy 4:2).

Third: "Feed My sheep." This is to say, make sure the mature ones get something to eat as well. When you deliver a message, it certainly needs to be accessible to everybody, including the baby Christians, but don't overlook the seasoned believers. We shepherds need to consistently include some nuggets of truth and insight that mature members of the flock can chew on.

As I finalize a message I've prepared, I consciously and intentionally ask myself if I've touched all of these bases. Of course, in order to do that you've got to put in significant amounts of sermon preparation time. I devote the greatest percentage of my working hours to preparing to feed, and feeding, the sheep. Indeed, it shocks most pastors to learn that I put more time into *feeding* than I do into *leading* (administrating).

Put simply, those two words describe my two main responsibilities as a shepherd. Sure, it's a complex role, but being a pastor really all boils down to *feed* and *lead*. If you're not interested in feeding and leading, you are probably not called to be senior pastor. And the main part of feeding the sheep consists of preaching.

I believe I have been gifted by God to preach and to teach. But like all raw gifts, they had to be developed and honed. For me, the development process involved carefully observing other effective preachers and teachers. I studied them like an aspiring golfer studies the swings of legendary players and asked why the most effective communicators of gospel truth did the things they did.

I also watched recordings of myself preaching. Which was painful—downright excruciating at times, actually. In my first couple of decades of ministry, I probably watched or listened to myself preach thousands of times. At first what stood out were the little nervous verbal tics and habits we all unconsciously exhibit when we speak in public.

I once shared this self-improvement technique with a pastor who had come to me for advice. His church simply hadn't grown, and he was looking for help. So I asked, "What do you learn when you listen to yourself preach." He made a sour face and said, "Oh no. I can't *stand* to hear myself preach!" My response was, "Well, neither can anyone else apparently. Perhaps that's the problem."

Believe me, I know it's awkward and disconcerting to listen to yourself, and doubly so to watch yourself—which allows you to be horrified by how you sound *and* how you look!

Several years ago when I was listening to myself teach, I noticed that I had developed the habit of preceding a thought with the phrase, "I want to tell you something…" Once I became aware of it, I noticed myself saying it again and again. It had become a verbal crutch. As I continued to listen, I couldn't believe how much I was repeating this phrase. Long before the message concluded, I found myself yelling at myself, "Just tell them already! They're listening!"

I walked away from that brutal listening session knowing I had a habit I needed to work on breaking if I was to become a more effective communicator. And effective communication of spiritual truth is essential to feeding sheep. So I worked on it.

Of course, I'm still working on becoming a better preacher. There's always room for improvement. Please understand, I'm not trying to be better than the next guy—I'm simply striving to be as good as I can possibly be.

If you're called to be a shepherd, I'm passionate about your being as good as you can be too. It's why I've written this book. Let me assure you, if you can communicate the Word of God well, you can grow a church. If you can feed sheep, sheep will come.

I remember having lunch with a gentleman who was acquainted with several pastors in my area. He told me, "You know, some pastors think you're a sheep stealer because so many of their people have left and now attend Gateway Church."

My response was, "I am *not* a sheep stealer. But I do plant delicious grass."

Frankly, if a family is in a church in which they are not being fed by the Word of God, my highest hope is that the shepherd there would begin feeding them. Absent that, I hope they *do* come to Gateway because I will feed those sheep. I'll watch over them. Pray for them. Equip them for success in life and ministry. In other words, I'll be a good shepherd.

I feed and lead. But if I had to choose only one as my top priority, I would say feeding is most important. I suspect many pastors would choose differently. Many would say that leading is a pastor's primary function. I disagree. Why? Because you cannot lead malnourished people into battle. You feed them and ensure that they grow to be strong, alert, and equipped. Then you have a group you can lead.

"Feed My sheep" is a life call from God for me.

13

Good Shepherds, False Shepherds, and Hirelings

WOULD YOU BELIEVE I ONCE LEARNED A LESSON about scattering sheep from a queen mother? Allow me to explain. Debbie and I were on a cruise and found ourselves sharing the beautiful ship and spectacular scenery with a large contingent of women belonging to a well-known national network of women's clubs—one distinguished by their brightly colored hats. It was some sort of floating national convention for this group.

Over the course of the cruise, I learned that the duly elected leader of each chapter is called a queen mother, and based upon my casual but curious observation that week, some of these queen mothers had allowed the title to go to their heads.

Debbie and I happened to be standing in line for a shore excursion one day, and we found one of these queen mothers standing behind us. How could I tell? Trust me. I could tell. She carried herself with a regal bearing as she held court with a small entourage. As a lifetime student of human nature and organizational dynamics, I really couldn't resist striking up a conversation.

I opened with, "Hey, I've never heard of the [Group Name] before this cruise. Please tell me about it."

She happily obliged, explaining that most cities have a chapter of this club and that each chapter has a leader, who is known as the queen mother. "She's the queen of that chapter," she explained. "As for me, I run a pretty tight ship," she continued. "I tell people, 'If you don't like the way we do things, you can go find another club or start your own!'"

I was intrigued at this point and followed up with another question. "So, how big is your chapter?" She said, "Oh, we have about fifteen people. We have new ladies join regularly, but it seems our group size always stays at a nice, manageable, intimate fifteen. Been that way for years."

My immediate thought was, *I think I know why.*

Over the years I have met some pastors with that queen-mother approach to shepherding. They tend to scatter the sheep. I can humbly but honestly say that I wish they would get out of the ministry and find another vocation. If you don't care about people and if you don't have a true shepherd's calling from God—if your heart doesn't burn to see people helped and fed and matured and equipped—you're doing no one any good, including yourself. If it's just a job to you, then it's time to quit!

The Bible has plenty to say about good shepherds. But it also has some pretty direct and sobering things to say about bad ones too. For example, the twenty-third chapter of Jeremiah brings us a stern warning about false shepherds:

> "Woe to the shepherds who destroy and scatter the sheep of My pasture!"
> says the LORD. Therefore thus says the LORD God of Israel against the
> shepherds who feed My people: "You have scattered My flock, driven
> them away, and not attended to them. Behold, I will attend to you for
> the evil of your doings," says the LORD. (Jeremiah 23:1–2)

Take special note of the word "scatter" in the passage above. This is a mark of a false pastor-shepherd. Invariably, their churches get smaller.

The number-one way to spot a false shepherd is a pattern of scattering sheep. Their churches get smaller, or at best stay the same size year after year. It always stuns me when I hear a pastor say something along the lines of, "Hey, if you don't like it here, go somewhere else." He clearly fails to realize that he is speaking to God's sheep, to God's own people.

Don't be a queen mother. Don't be the guy who says, "It's my way or the highway." That's not shepherd-style leadership. The fact is, it must be God's way, not your way.

This is not to suggest that a pastor should be negligent in keeping an eye out for individuals in the church who are troublemakers or wolves in sheep's clothing. In such a case, you quietly pull such people aside and insist that they leave. It is something else entirely to stand in the pulpit and tell the entire congregation, "Hey, people, you can leave if you don't like the way I'm doing things." That will scatter God's people.

Take another look at those verses. Note whose pasture it actually is being tended by the false shepherd. God said, "Woe to the shepherds who destroy and scatter the sheep of *My pasture*." Who owns these sheep? God does!

Now note to whom God directed His comments. He spoke "against the shepherds who feed My people." As we've already seen, a shepherd's sacred, fundamental role is to *feed* and *lead*.

Finally, give your attention to what God said to these sheep-scattering false shepherds: "Behold, I will attend to you."

I don't know about you, but those are words I never want to hear from God. Can you imagine what Judgment Day will be like for false shepherds? for people who have hurt God's own sheep? It makes the hair on the back of my neck stand up to think about it.

So, what is God's remedy for the problem of false shepherds? He'll find good shepherds for His sheep:

"But I will gather the remnant of My flock out of all countries where
I have driven them, and bring them back to their folds; and they shall
be fruitful and increase. I will set up shepherds over them who will feed
them; and they shall fear no more, nor be dismayed, nor shall they be
lacking," says the LORD. (verses 3–4)

God said He will "set up shepherds…*who will feed them*." As we see again and again in the Word, a shepherd's highest and most basic duty is to feed the sheep.

Yes, many churches are languishing because they are headed by false shepherds operating from wrong motives. But that's not the only reason for failure. I think there are also many true shepherds who are simply in the wrong position in the church structure.

For example, if you're not gifted to preach, you probably shouldn't be a senior pastor (or one that has primary pulpit responsibilities). This doesn't mean you don't have a true shepherd's heart. It just means that heart should probably be expressed in a role within the church structure that doesn't have sheep feeding as its primary task.

Of course, good shepherds do more than feed. Jesus gives us a broader picture of the pastor-shepherd's role in the tenth chapter of John. Indeed, the entire chapter is about being a shepherd. There we learn that vigilant, self-sacrificing protection of the sheep comes naturally to the true shepherd.

In John 10:11–12 Jesus declared, "I am the good shepherd. The good shepherd gives His life for the sheep. But a hireling, he who is not the shepherd, one who does not own the sheep, sees the wolf coming and leaves the sheep and flees; and the wolf catches the sheep and scatters them."

ᵥᶑ Keys to a Blessed Church

I think there are also many *true* shepherds who are simply in the wrong position in the church structure.

There are different kinds of service, but the same Lord. There are different kinds of working, but the same God works all of them in all men. Now to each one the manifestation of the Spirit is given for the common good. (1 Corinthians 12:5–7, NIV)

A pastor-shepherd has to be willing to lay his life down for the sheep. It's a spiritually dangerous world out there. The Enemy of their souls is prowling around looking for the weak, the young, the vulnerable, and the ailing; he'll devour them at every opportunity (see 1 Peter 5:8). The true shepherd recognizes this and stands vigilant in watching over the sheep. He'll fight for them— sacrificing comfort and sleep to protect them.

The hireling flees because it's just a job to him. Jesus declares that He is not a hireling. And as we're about to learn, those He calls don't think or respond like hirelings either.

14

The True Shepherd's Call

THERE IS A WONDERFUL PROPHETIC PROMISE in the third chapter of Jeremiah. There the Lord speaks of a future day of blessing and favor. It's the day in which we're living: "And I will give you shepherds according to My heart, who will feed you with knowledge and understanding" (Jeremiah 3:15).

There are two truths implied in this verse. One implication is that true shepherds are a blessing from the Lord to His people. The other is that there are shepherds out there who are *not* shepherding in accordance with God's heart.

Jesus warns about false shepherds in the gospel of John:

"Most assuredly, I say to you, he who does not enter the sheepfold by the door, but climbs up some other way, the same is a thief and a robber. But he who enters by the door is the shepherd of the sheep. To him the door-keeper opens, and the sheep hear his voice; and he calls his own sheep by name and leads them out. And when he brings out his own sheep, he goes before them; and the sheep follow him, for they know his voice. Yet they will by no means follow a stranger, but will flee from him, for they do not know the voice of strangers." Jesus used this illustration, but they did not understand the things which He spoke to them. (10:1–6)

In Jesus's illustration, the sheepfold is the church. He describes one who tries to gain access to the sheep through a way other than the door (in a moment we'll learn what that door represents). He goes on to say that the one who doesn't enter by the door, but rather climbs up some other way, is "a thief and a robber."

A few verses later, Jesus reiterates that "the thief does not come except to steal, and to kill, and to destroy" (John 10:10). Here Jesus makes it clear that the false shepherd is actually doing the work of Satan.

And what about the good shepherds—the ones Jeremiah prophesied would shepherd in accordance with God's own heart? Jesus had some thoughts about these in this discourse as well. It is clear that as He speaks of the good shepherd, Jesus is speaking first and foremost of Himself (He said so explicitly in verses 11 and 14). But these characteristics will also apply to those who are called by the Good Shepherd to serve as under-shepherds.

Jesus gives us several key marks that characterize the ministry of a true shepherd. Notice that He says, "To him the doorkeeper opens, and the sheep hear his voice; and he calls his own sheep by name and *leads them out*. And when he brings out his own sheep, *he goes before them;* and the sheep follow him, for they know his voice" (verses 3–4).

Note that Jesus *leads* His sheep by going *before* them. He's not standing behind them, shouting and driving them with a whip. He's not driving them before Him by poking them with sharp sticks. He's in front of them with His shepherd's staff. He demonstrates the path. In other words, the true shepherd models where he wants the sheep to go. He leads by example.

There's a powerful lesson for pastors in that. By the way, the shepherd's staff is for fighting off wolves and other wild predators, not for beating the sheep. True shepherds lead the sheep and fight the enemy.

Did you notice John's little commentary at the end of Jesus's discourse on true and false shepherds? It's in verse 6: "Jesus used this illustration, but they did not understand the things which He spoke to them." How did John know? Because he was one of the "they" that didn't understand. Probably seeing the bewildered looks on His disciples' faces, Jesus makes His point explicit:

> Then Jesus said to them again, "Most assuredly, I say to you, I am the
> door of the sheep. All who ever came before Me are thieves and robbers,
> but the sheep did not hear them. I am the door." (verses 7–9)

Anyone who tries to be a shepherd without coming through Jesus is illegitimate and destructive. Which means that only Jesus can call and gift true shepherds. You must be called by Jesus to be a shepherd.

This is not speaking solely of senior pastors. This truth applies to all who function as shepherds, particularly those on the pastoral staff. Even lay leaders in the church frequently function as shepherds. But none can receive that calling except through Jesus.

Of course, Jesus does call some to be senior pastors, but not many. Still, many individuals function as associate pastors who aspire to become senior pastors. In some cases it's because they see the appealing, attractive side of functioning in that office. They see the attention, the higher income, the prestige, or the perks. What they don't see as clearly is the weight, the pressure, and the burdens. (To be honest, the burdens outweigh the perks.)

That's why you should only seek the role of senior pastor if you're sure you've been called to it. Supernatural grace and enabling come to those who have been truly called by the Great Shepherd. But without that grace, it can be brutal. I encourage associate pastors to thrive in that vital and fulfilling role until they are absolutely sure they have been called and are ready to be a senior pastor.

This message tends to hurt some feelings and ruffle some feathers. This is America after all. We've been conditioned to view every organization as a corporate ladder that must be climbed until we reach the top. In our worldview, every Number Two must aspire to be Number One. But this is a trap. If it's not your calling to serve as a senior pastor, you don't want to do it.

⮢ Keys to a Blessed Church

The true shepherd models where he wants the sheep to go. He leads by example.

Follow my example, as I follow the example of Christ. (1 Corinthians 11:1, NIV)

One of the many things I admire about Gateway's Tom Lane—my Number Two—is that he knows what he's called and equipped by God to do, and he does it at an extraordinarily high level. He's studied the role. He's thought and prayed deeply about it. I believe he's taken that role to places few have ever imagined. But none of that would have happened if he had fallen for the deception that everyone is called to be a senior pastor. (Actually, I'm not the Number One at Gateway Church. I'm Number Two. Number One died for me.)

I can assure you that I would not be offended in the least if you said to me, "Pastor Robert, you have no business aspiring to be a worship leader. I love you, but that's just not your gift." I would be okay with that. True, leading worship *does* look fun. Yes, it would be very cool to lead people into God's presence where they can be touched and changed and made whole. But I know I'm not gifted—naturally or spiritually—to do that.

So, why does it hurt people's feelings when you tell them they can't preach? Preaching is a gift too. Many think that if they just work hard enough at it, they can become inspiring, effective preachers. That's simply not the case.

There is nothing better than finding your place—the role that God has called and gifted you to thrive in. Some senior pastors have been struggling and floundering for decades. I hate to be the one to break this to them, but it may not be resistance from the devil that's producing a lack of results. It is likely that they might be in the wrong position. It is more than likely that they would make the best associate pastors in the world. Oh, how I would love to see all the believers in the body of Christ find their God-ordained places!

Over the years of Gateway's existence, a remarkable number of former senior pastors have joined our staff as associate pastors. Some of them had been utterly miserable in the senior pastor role, but then came to Gateway and began thriving. (In chapter 20, I'll share with you how we facilitate this through empowerment.)

This isn't to suggest that there aren't some associate pastors who *are* called to be senior pastors; they are trained and equipped by the Lord in the associate role for a season before being set into their long-term role. For example, one of the very first full-time staff hires I made after I launched Gateway was a spiritually gifted man named Brady Boyd. In his six years at Gateway, he performed a number of pastoral functions, including serving as our first small-groups pastor. He excelled at them all.

Eventually it became very clear to me that Brady was called to be a senior pastor. In fact, based on some conversations we've had, I may have known it before he did. In his final couple of years at Gateway, I had him preach numerous times at our main weekend services. On two occasions when I was scheduled to be out of the pulpit for four consecutive weeks, I had Brady preach during my entire absence, even though we had a number of other gifted and able preachers on staff.

Although I didn't mention it to Brady at the time, the Lord had shown me that Brady had a strong calling to be a senior pastor, and I was being intentional about preparing and equipping him.

Then in 2007, a wonderful and influential church in Colorado Springs—New Life Church—entered a season of crisis when its high-profile senior pastor was caught in a very public moral failure. That pastor resigned, and New Life entered a difficult season of turmoil, heartache, and confusion. Eventually the pulpit search committee of the church reached out to a group of pastors that included Jimmy Evans. That process resulted in a search that ended with the unanimous, enthusiastic selection of Brady to be the new senior pastor at New Life Church.

That congregation has thrived under Brady's shepherding—even through some extraordinary trials. For example, only a few months after Brady took the position there, a troubled young man with a gun walked into the lobby of New Life and began shooting as the Sunday services were winding down. He killed two teenage girls and wounded three others before being shot by a security guard.

By that evening the nation was seeing Brady on Fox News and CNN and other news services as he faced an army of microphones and cameras. It was a crisis no senior pastor could possibly imagine facing, yet Brady handled it with grace, poise, and most importantly, Spirit-led wisdom.

I'm not congratulating myself when I say that I saw that Brady Boyd was called to be a senior pastor. It was evident. But that's not always the case. The key is to be sure of our calling. And whatever we do, only access the sheepfold through the Door. To try to climb up some other way is to become a destructive thief.

15

The Shepherd Loves the Sheep

ANY STUDENT OF THE BIBLE IS LIKELY FAMILIAR with the gifts of the Holy Spirit. Pastors may differ among themselves about their use and relevance for today, but all could probably tell you what they are. (For my views on the gifts and lots of other aspects of the person and work of the Holy Spirit, please see my book *The God I Never Knew: How Real Friendship with the Holy Spirit Can Change Your Life.*)

But when I stand before a group of pastors and ask them, "Do you believe in the gifts of Jesus?" I usually just get blank stares. *The gifts of Jesus?* Actually, we find Paul discussing these gifts in the letter to the Ephesians:

> But to each one of us grace was given according to the measure of Christ's gift.... And He Himself gave some to be apostles, some prophets, some evangelists, and some pastors and teachers, for the equipping of the saints for the work of ministry, for the edifying of the body of Christ. (4:7, 11–12)

The gifts of Jesus to the church are gifts of ministers—apostles, prophets, evangelists, pastors, and teachers. But as Paul revealed here, all of these *ministers* have the same *ministry.* That ministry is "equipping." Now, that equipping ministry manifests in differing ways among those five offices, but they all are given to produce the same outcome: to equip the saints for the work of ministry and to edify (or strengthen) the body of Christ.

This revelation shows us how to spot a true shepherd: he is an equipper. He is able and eager to equip people to do the work of the ministry.

The fact is, Jesus loves the sheep. Hebrews 13:20 calls Him "that great

Shepherd of the sheep." First Peter 2:25 calls Him "the Shepherd and Overseer" of our souls. And I love the window into the heart of Jesus we get in Mark 6:34:

> And Jesus, when He came out, saw a great multitude and was moved
> with compassion for them, because they were like sheep not having a
> shepherd. So He began to teach them many things.

When the desire to shepherd lost sheep rose up in the Son of God, what did He do to give expression to that compassion? He fed them. "So He began to teach them many things."

The life of a true shepherd is not an easy one. It's not for the faint of heart. And it's certainly not for the selfish. In fact, as Jesus made clear in John chapter 10, the calling will cost you your life:

> I am the good shepherd; and I know My sheep, and am known by
> My own. As the Father knows Me, even so I know the Father; and
> I lay down My life for the sheep. (verses 14–15)

There's no way around it. Being a true shepherd requires a constant dying to self. It's going to cost you your life. There is an ominous but wonderful passage in Ezekiel that not only deals with this truth but also contains an amazing, little-known prophecy about the Great Shepherd to come:

> Therefore, you shepherds, hear the word of the LORD: "As I live," says
> the Lord GOD, "surely because My flock became a prey, and My flock
> became food for every beast of the field, because there was no shepherd,
> nor did My shepherds search for My flock, but the shepherds fed them-
> selves and did not feed My flock"—therefore, O shepherds, hear the
> word of the LORD! Thus says the Lord GOD: "Behold, I am against the
> shepherds." (Ezekiel 34:7–10)

Once again God is speaking through His prophet to condemn false shepherds. In this case, the indictment against the spiritual shepherds of Judah is that they "fed themselves and did not feed My flock." Are you beginning to get the picture that feeding the sheep is a big deal to God? Furthermore, in this case the shepherds put their own needs above the needs of the sheep. God takes a dim view of this. "Behold, I am against the shepherds."

But there is more in this passage. Just a few verses later, Ezekiel wrote,

For thus says the Lord GOD: "Indeed I Myself will search for My sheep and seek them out. As a shepherd seeks out his flock on the day he is among his scattered sheep, so will I seek out My sheep and deliver them from all the places where they were scattered on a cloudy and dark day." (verses 11–12)

This is a messianic prophecy. It speaks of the coming of Jesus who came "as a shepherd seeks out...[His] scattered sheep." Notice what the prophecy says about the sheep's scattering and their day of deliverance. It was a "cloudy and dark day."

ᴈᴈ Keys to a Blessed Church

> Here's a surefire way to spot a true shepherd: he is an equipper. He is able and eager to equip people to do the work of the ministry.
>
> Their responsibility is to equip God's people to do his work and build up the church, the body of Christ. (Ephesians 4:12, NLT)

Can you think of a notable day in the life of Jesus in which the skies grew cloudy and the sun became darkened? Of course, I'm referring to the day of Jesus's crucifixion—the day the Great Shepherd became the spotless, worthy Lamb, sacrificed for the sins of the world (see Luke 23:45).

That's the Great Shepherd's heart. And the most awesome responsibility we pastors have is to shepherd His sheep.

16

Your First and Most
Important Ministry

THIS COULD EASILY HAVE BEEN THE FIRST CHAPTER in this section rather than the final one. It is certainly no less important than any that have preceded it. Indeed, it describes the most important stewardship responsibility any married pastor-shepherd has.

Obviously, I'm referring to the role of spouse and parent. And for the overwhelming majority of pastors reading this book, that is the role of husband and father.

Moses—the great shepherd of Israel who led an enormous flock of God's people out of bondage and into the land of promise—is one of the towering figures in the Bible. He figures enormously in God's grand, unfolding plan of redemption that culminated in the birth, death, and resurrection of Jesus Christ. And yet when it came to being a husband and father, he is an example of terrific failure.

The book of Exodus provides ample evidence of this. In chapter 4, for example, we find Moses on the way back to Egypt after forty years of working with his father-in-law Jethro as a shepherd. He had encountered the Lord at the burning bush, received his instructions to act as God's deliverer of His people, and seen his shepherd's staff commissioned as an instrument of God's power (see Exodus 3).

As Moses, along with his wife Zipporah and their two sons, headed back to Egypt, a very strange incident took place:

And it came to pass on the way, at the encampment, that the LORD met him and sought to kill him. Then Zipporah took a sharp stone and cut off the foreskin of her son and cast it at Moses' feet, and said, "Surely you are a husband of blood to me!" So He let him go. Then she said, "You are a husband of blood!"—because of the circumcision. (Exodus 4:24–26)

Now Moses wrote the first five books of the Bible, including this passage in Exodus, so he's writing about something he personally experienced. But he doesn't provide us with a lot of detail here. Indeed he's fairly matter-of-fact about the whole episode. It's basically, "Yeah, God showed up planning to kill me. Then my wife circumcised our son with a sharp rock, yelled at me, and then threw the foreskin at me. You know…because of that whole circumcision thing. And then the next day…"

We can only imagine how disconcerting it must be to have the God of the Universe stroll into Moses's campsite on a mission to kill him. I suppose if that happened to me I'd probably try to skim over it as quickly as possible too.

✑ Keys to a Blessed Church

Pastors, we cannot sacrifice our families on the altar of ministry. We must be good husbands and fathers first. We can't be truly blessed leaders any other way.

For if a man cannot manage his own household, how can he take care of God's church? (1 Timothy 3:5, NLT)

Why had Moses fallen out of favor with God? Because Moses was carrying some instructions from God for the Israelites that included a command to reinstitute the covenant sign of circumcision among the people. Yet Moses's own sons had not been circumcised. In other words, he was about to start preaching something he wasn't living out in his own family.

Zipporah hadn't bought into the meaning and importance of circumcision as a sign of covenant. She hadn't embraced it because Moses clearly hadn't explained it to her. At least not very well. (Obviously, when your wife starts flinging bloody foreskins at you, what you have there is a failure to communicate!)

Moses hadn't taken the time to teach his own family the ways of God. But I can't throw stones. I recall a quiet evening earlier in our marriage when Debbie, out of nowhere, said, "Robert, will you do something for me?"

"Of course, honey," was my reply. "What do you need?"

"Well, as long as I've known you, you've heard the voice of God so clearly. Do you think…if you have time…? I know you're busy, but do you think you could teach me how to hear God like you do?"

At first, I was stunned. Since the first day we met as teenagers, Debbie had been one of the most spiritual, godly people I'd ever known. I suppose I had always just assumed that she heard God's voice with the same clarity and detail that I did. Quickly my surprise gave way to profound conviction.

God forgive me, I thought. *I've traveled all over this country for years teaching other people how to hear the voice of God. I've led seminars and college classes on the subject. And I haven't taken the time to minister that wonderful, life-transforming truth to my own wife!*

Moses made that same mistake: After the confrontation over circumcision, Moses sent his wife and sons back to stay with her father (see Exodus 18:1–6). They didn't accompany Moses back to Egypt. Think about it, they missed one of the greatest seasons of miracles and wonders human eyes have ever witnessed.

They missed seeing the plagues that brought mighty Egypt to its knees. They missed the immensely meaningful night of the Passover, in which the angel of death passed over every Israelite house that had the blood of the lamb painted on the doorposts. This was the event that prophetically foreshadowed a Passover night thirty-five hundred years in the future when the shed blood of the Lamb of God would break death's hold on believing mankind forever. They missed the Israelites' glorious and joyful departure from Egypt, carrying the gold of Egypt away as restitution for four hundred years of forced labor. They missed seeing the Red Sea open for the massive horde of tribes and then seeing it swallow the Egyptian armies. They missed being led by the pillars of fire and cloud.

When it came time for the Israelites to finally possess the land of promise, Moses's two boys weren't there with Joshua and Caleb winning victories and taking cities.

What a shame! Moses's family wasn't with him in his ministry. Something very similar can happen with ministers today. It's not uncommon for a wife to be sitting on the front row while her husband preaches but not be truly with him in ministry. I've seen children of evangelists grow up with their dad in the ministry—he's winning thousands to Christ, but his kids fail to enter the Promised Land.

Moses was a gifted and accomplished leader of people—by God's grace, one of the greatest the world has ever seen. But he failed in his most vital leadership role: he sacrificed his family for the ministry. That's not God's will! And yet it happens time and time again in ministry.

I know because I came dangerously close to losing my own family. In my case, it happened when my ministry had really only just gotten started. As my congregation has heard me testify on many occasions, I was a profoundly immoral young man growing up—even though I had wonderful, godly parents who did their best to raise me well. I rebelled against much of what they and the church stood for, exposing myself to a great deal of uncleanness that included alcohol, profanity, drug abuse, and sexual promiscuity.

When I was barely sixteen, in spite of my self-destructive background and the fact that I was lost and bound for hell, a sweet, godly girl named Debbie saw something in me. A few years later, for reasons I cannot fathom to this very day, she agreed to marry me. And even more inexplicably, her normally sensible parents allowed it.

Around that same time, a traveling evangelist saw something in me as well and hired me to help with his crusades. At that point, even though I was lost, I had a faith-filled wife praying for me, and I was routinely being confronted with the message of the gospel. The proverbial hound of heaven was on my heels, and my days of running from God were rapidly coming to an end.

One night, in a small, roadside inn called Jake's Motel, I knelt beside the bed and surrendered my life to God. I was instantly and gloriously saved. I can say with all sincerity that nothing in my life from that day forward has ever been the same.

Nevertheless, as I've learned over the years, experiencing forgiveness and walking in complete freedom are two different things in the Christian life. Forgiveness was instantaneous, but because of my background, I still had a number of physical and mental habits that clung to me in my new life. I didn't know then what I know now about how our birthright in Jesus allows us to appropriate freedom from demonic strongholds. What's more, I entered full-time ministry almost immediately after being saved. I had scarcely gotten up off my knees before I was preaching at youth revivals and experiencing significant and growing success. Of course, the apostle Paul warns against putting young believers in the ministry limelight for a reason. Within months, I had a catastrophic moral failure. To be specific, I committed a grievous betrayal of my marriage vows.

After being caught and then confronted by my pastor, I confessed to my devastated wife and submitted myself to the elders of the church I was attending. I stepped away from ministry for an extended season of counseling, freedom ministry, and restoration. My priority was not to save my ministry but to save my young marriage. I'm unspeakably blessed to be able to report that, by God's grace and my precious wife's tenacity, both were healed and restored beyond my wildest dreams.

I've had twenty-five wonderful, faithful, blissful years with the wife of my youth since that restoration process. Together we've raised three children who are all in love with Jesus and serving in ministry in one form or another.

Looking back, I can see that I was just a kid when I opened the door to the destroyer. But I never cease to be grateful that the Enemy wasn't able to wreck my most important ministry assignment—my family—before it had even begun.

Pastors, we cannot sacrifice our families on the altar of ministry. We must be good husbands and fathers first. We can't be truly blessed leaders any other way.

PART 4

Blessed Leaders

17

Who's the Minister Here?

WHO ARE THE MINISTERS IN YOUR CHURCH? Ask the typical believer in the typical pew to identify the minister, and ninety-nine times out of a hundred you'll find a finger pointed at the pastor. Ask the pastor that question, and he's likely to point in the same direction—toward himself. Here's the thing about that: I don't believe that was God's intention for the local church at all.

Today there are basically two ways to do church—the traditional way and the biblical way.

In the traditional model, the job of ministering to people falls to us "professionals." In this paradigm, the "regular" folks (lay people) come to church to be ministered to by the pastor, and if the church is large enough, by the other pros on the staff. On the weekend, the lay people come to receive ministry from the pulpit. And if they need prayer, encouragement, spiritual support, or anything else during the week, the pastor is expected to address those needs too. This is the root cause of pastor burnout, as we'll see in a later chapter.

So, how does the biblical model differ? I'm convinced that God intends those sitting in the pews (or chairs, as the case may be) to be the ministers—ministers to the world, to be exact. And the pastor's job is to equip them for ministry. In other words, the pastor, along with the other Christians on the church staff, are the *equippers*.

But few churches today actually operate that way. To validate that view, let me take you back to Moses and expand upon the theme established in the previous chapter.

Going back to the book of Exodus, we find Moses operating in the traditional model—one man trying to minister to and meet the needs of a large congregation. Moses's father-in-law, Jethro, is standing by watching the whole operation:

> And so it was, on the next day, that Moses sat to judge the people; and
> the people stood before Moses from morning until evening. So when
> Moses' father-in-law saw all that he did for the people, he said, "What
> is this thing that you are doing for the people? Why do you alone sit,
> and all the people stand before you from morning until evening?"
>
> And Moses said to his father-in-law, "Because the people come to
> me to inquire of God. When they have a difficulty, they come to me,
> and I judge between one and another; and I make known the statutes
> of God and His laws." (18:13–16)

You'll recall that Jethro was essentially a successful rancher in Midian (see Exodus 3:1). He ran an operation that managed large flocks of sheep, goats, and other livestock. In other words, he knew a little about being a shepherd. And he knew that once your flocks grow to a certain size, you're doomed if you don't learn how to delegate. As a matter of fact, originally Jethro had hired Moses on as an associate shepherd after Moses had fled Egypt.

One day, as Moses and the Israelites were camping in the wilderness, Jethro came for a visit. He took one look at Moses's approach to pastoring, diagnosed the fatal flaw, and wrote him a prescription:

> So Moses' father-in-law said to him, "The thing that you do is *not good.*
> Both you and these people who are *with you will surely wear yourselves
> out.* For this thing is too much for you; you are not able to perform it by
> yourself. Listen now to my voice; I will give you counsel, and God will
> be with you: Stand before God for the people, so that you may bring the
> difficulties to God. And you shall teach them the statutes and the laws,
> and show them the way in which they must walk and the work they

must do. Moreover you shall select from all the people able men, such as fear God, men of truth, hating covetousness; and place such over them to be rulers of thousands, rulers of hundreds, rulers of fifties, and rulers of tens. And let them judge the people at all times. Then it will be that every great matter they shall bring to you, but every small matter they themselves shall judge. So it will be easier for you, for they will bear the burden with you. If you do this thing, and God so commands you, then you will be able to endure, and all this people will also go to their place in peace." (Exodus 18:17–23)

Clearly a master of understatement, Jethro took one look at the leadership approach that was so dysfunctional that it was driving Moses to pray for God to just kill him and pronounced it "not good."

He explained that this model of ministry would not only exhaust Moses but the people as well. "Both you and these people who are with you will surely wear yourselves out" (verse 17). I've seen this syndrome operating in many churches.

It wears out the pastor for obvious reasons. There is no way he can possibly address the ministry needs of every member. But it also wears the members out because they are looking to him for things he cannot possibly deliver. That's a failed model of ministry, but it has been the predominant model for centuries.

Prior to the Reformation, we had priests in sole possession of the Word of God and a largely illiterate membership utterly dependent upon the clergy for understanding of God's will and ways. The thought of the laity being involved in ministry would have been more than shocking. It would have been heresy.

The Reformation eroded this distinction but didn't eliminate it. The dominant paradigm continued to be that the role of the clergy was to offer ministry and the role of the congregants was to receive it.

The twentieth century brought a wave of fresh understanding of the gifts God places in His people for the express purpose of blessing others and demonstrating the power of the gospel.

Nevertheless, the church is extremely inwardly focused right now, and this is not—and has never been—God's intent. Jesus wasn't self-absorbed when He walked the earth. We, His body, can't be either if we are going to accurately display Him to a lost and dying world. It's great that lay people are now involved in ministry, but in many cases that ministry is exclusively directed toward other believers and still takes place within the four walls of the church. The full expression of God's plan for His New Covenant people is every believer expressing in powerful ways the fullness of the Spirit's gifts in the home, the marketplace, the workplace, and on the street—so that the lost will be reached and touched.

⤳ Keys to a Blessed Church

> The church is extremely inwardly focused right now and that has never been God's intent. Jesus wasn't self-absorbed when He walked the earth. We, His body, can't be either if we are going to accurately display Him to a lost and dying world.
>
> > And He Himself gave some to be apostles, some prophets, some evangelists, and some pastors and teachers, for the equipping of the saints for the work of ministry, for the edifying of the body of Christ. (Ephesians 4:11–12)

Every believer is called to be a minister. Paul said we have all been made "able ministers" of the New Covenant (2 Corinthians 3:6, KJV).

God has deposited gifts within every member of your congregation. The highest fulfillment and joy they can experience can only be found by using those gifts for the advancement of God's purposes—in them and in the world. Believers cannot be truly happy or at peace as long as they remain largely focused upon themselves and their own needs, wants, and hurts. Only in becoming outwardly focused on ministering to the needs of others can they experience real satisfaction and sense of purpose. Thus we pastors do them a great disservice if we allow people to continue to see themselves primarily as *recipients* of ministry rather than *deliverers* of ministry.

18

The Pastor's Three-Part Job Description

HERE ARE A FEW FACTS FOR YOUR CONSIDERATION: According to The Barna Group, roughly 60 percent of the Protestant churches in the United States have fewer than 100 hundred members and a full 98 percent have fewer than 1000. In other words, small churches are the rule, not the exception. At the same time, we have become an increasingly urban nation. That means our population is increasingly concentrated in major cities as fewer people live in small towns. In fact, in 2010 more than 82 percent of Americans lived in an urban or suburban area, according to the CIA's World Factbook.

I mention these numbers because they reveal something about the failure of our churches to effectively reach out in our communities. Clearly, not every church can grow to have tens of thousands of members. If a church in a community of 3,000 souls grows to a membership of 300, that body is actually reaching and (we hope) discipling 10 percent of its harvest field. Gateway Church is located on the northern edge of the Dallas-Fort Worth Metroplex—an area that is home to more than 6.7 million people. If we were discipling 10 percent of that harvest field, our membership would be 670,000 people. We currently have some distance to travel before we're there!

Nevertheless, I believe there is a reason the average church size in this increasingly urbanized nation is well below two hundred: the vast majority of pastors and congregations are still operating under that old, flawed paradigm of the pastor's role. Put another way, we're still running our churches like Moses was running the First Church of the Israelites when he became so exasperated that he prayed for God to kill him.

In other words, if, as the pastor, I'm the only one whose job it is to marry, bury, counsel, visit the hospitalized, encourage those in nursing homes or homebound, evangelize the lost, pray for the downcast and oppressed, and exhort the weary, then I'm quickly going to become worn out, discouraged, and cynical. And guess what? Many pastors are worn out, discouraged, and cynical.

So, just what *is* your job as a pastor? Let's return to Moses and his wise management consultant, Jethro, for some spiritual insight into the answer. There we'll find three essential tasks at the heart of an effective, balanced pastor's role.

1. PRAY

Jethro was appalled at the way Moses was shepherding his enormous flock. Just how large was that flock? Most conservative Bible scholars estimate the size of the Israelite nation participating in the exodus to be somewhere between 1.6 million and 3 million individuals. Let's just assume for a moment that there were 2 million people in the camp. That's a big church.

As an aside, the Bible tells us that when the Israelites miraculously passed through the Red Sea on their way out of Egypt, it was a type and forerunner of baptism. I suppose that means Moses could have shown up at the pastors' conference later on and boasted that his church had baptized two million people in the past year! Pastoring a church of two million may have been good for his reputation back at denominational headquarters, but it was bad for his family, bad for his health, and bad for his members.

In any event, as we've seen, Jethro took one look at the self-imposed job description Moses was operating under and declared it crazy. He then proceeded to offer his son-in-law some wise advice from an old master shepherd. It remains sound advice for pastors today. First, Jethro said, "Listen now to my voice; I will give you counsel, and God will be with you: *Stand before God for the people,* so that you may bring the difficulties to God" (Exodus 18:19).

The first item of correction Moses received about his job description was essentially this: *Represent the people to God.* We have a handy word in English for this activity: *intercession.* Jethro told Moses to stop spending all his time (literally, from sunup to sundown) trying to solve everyone's problems. Instead, he needed to take their problems to God in prayer!

Also notice that the advice was *not* to stand before the people for God. Yet this is precisely what many pastors view as their principal role. They think their first job priority is to represent God to the people, when in reality the most vital thing a pastor can do is represent his people to God.

As if to remove any doubt about this in Moses's mind, Jethro explained that the purpose of standing before God on the congregation's behalf is "so that you may bring the [peoples'] difficulties to God."

By the way, this is prayer in its rawest, most basic form. It is simply taking our needs, burdens, and difficulties to God...and leaving them there. (If you don't leave them there, you haven't really prayed. You've just griped in God's presence.) Likewise, intercession is the act of bringing someone else's need, burdens, or difficulties to Him—and leaving them there.

Spending time in the presence of God is the first and most vital element in the pastor's job description. But may I tell you with great sadness that this is frequently the last thing many pastors are allowed to do? Pastors have some of the thinnest, puniest prayer lives I've ever seen. And often it's not really their fault. They're expected to be involved in every aspect of ministry in the church— run every meeting, visit every family, solve every problem, and personally meet every need.

Think about it. How would many deacon boards, oversight committees, and self-appointed church bosses react if their pastor started spending half of each day alone in his office with his phone turned off?

Their expectations are built upon the traditional paradigm of the pastor's role. It is a view that assumes that a pastor must meet with every person who expresses an interest in meeting with him. And the result is that the last person he ever gets to meet with is God!

In my own life and ministry, I have had to fight to make the shift away from this. I can attest that it does require a fight. Often the fight is with my own soul because I love people. I want to help people. And I want them to be happy with me. So, I have to build time with God into my schedule as a sacred priority. And I have to constantly remind myself *and* those around me that the best, most effective, and most powerful way I can help the members of our body is to stand before God on their behalf. If you could see my electronic day planner, you would immediately note that out of my regular fifty-hour work week, time for study and prayer occupy more hours than any other activity. It must be so.

That's why you will not find me agreeing to meet with every member who requests time with me. I will politely and tactfully refer them to another member of the pastoral staff. I'm not being elitist or snobby. Nor am I being lazy. I've just learned that the moment I let the daily demands of the people or the ministry begin eroding my time with God, I have begun to surrender the Source of greatest positive impact on both.

What form do my times of prayer take? I routinely pray for the elders of our church. I pray over the staff and their families. I pray for the children, the marriages within our body, the financial health of our families, for every individual connected to our church, and whatever else the Holy Spirit brings to my mind.

Often in prayer I'll see the faces of members of our congregation. Sometimes I know the name that goes with that face, and other times I don't. But I'll take it as a cue to lift up that person to the Lord. From time to time I will take a printout of our church's membership list and call out the names of families as He draws my attention to them. I cry out, "Lord, strengthen this marriage. Prosper this family. Reveal yourself to them in power and grace. Bless them!"

When I do this, I am functioning at the heart of my role as a senior pastor: not representing God to the people but *representing the people to God.*

❧ Keys to a Blessed Church

I'm not being elitist or snobby. Nor am I being lazy. I've just learned that the moment I let the daily demands of the people or the ministry begin eroding my time with God, I have begun to surrender the Source of greatest positive impact on both.

> Moreover, as for me, far be it from me that I should sin against the LORD in ceasing to pray for you; but I will teach you the good and the right way. (1 Samuel 12:23)

2. TEACH THE WORD

Praying for the people was only the first element in Jethro's three-pronged pastoral job description for Moses. We find the second one in Exodus 18:20: "And you shall teach them the statutes and the laws, and show them the way in which they must walk and the work they must do."

As I've spoken to hundreds of pastors over the last ten years, I've been consistently shocked to discover how little time many of them are able to spend preparing to teach the Word.

In most cases, it's not their fault. Once again, it's the mode of doing church (and the paradigm that produces it) that is to blame. The expectation of the congregation is "Bring us life-changing fresh bread and meat each weekend, but also make sure you're in the office all week long, taking phone calls, running meetings, and personally administrating every aspect of the church." It's an impossible, irreconcilable set of expectations.

I recall speaking with one pastor who was frustrated at his church's lack of growth and his membership's lack of maturity. I asked him about his sermon preparation. He told me he usually prepared his sermon in a couple of hours on Saturday night. After reading the stunned expression on my face, he added, "It's the only available time I have!"

I've learned that a fundamental part of my role as a pastor is to spend a significant percentage of my working time each week studying and preparing to deliver the Word on the weekend so the people can be equipped for ministry. (Remember, feed the sheep!) Other than representing the people to God in prayer, there is no higher priority. And there is no other activity I can undertake that will bear greater fruit in ministry. It's vital.

Take another look at Jethro's instruction to Moses. He encouraged him to teach the people God's statutes and "show them the way in which they must walk and the work they must do."

Jethro specifically outlined two key areas of focus for Moses's teaching ministry:

1. the way they must walk (character)
2. the work they must do (ministry)

That is a pretty good road map for balanced preaching and teaching: the *way* and the *work*.

If I only bring messages that focus on character—the inner life of believers and their behavior—I am missing part of the equation. From time to time I must also preach and teach the truth about what we believers are supposed to be doing out there in the world. After all, as we've seen, the pastor's job description is *equipping the people for ministry.*

A few years ago I went on retreat and spent some time evaluating my preaching in the light of this revelation. It was clear to me that up to that point the overwhelming majority of my messages could be categorized as "the way we must walk" sermons. I asked the Lord if I had done my congregation a disservice. He reassured me that I hadn't. He said, *You have to make sure people know the way they should walk before they set out on the work they must do.* But He also assured me that He was bringing this truth to my attention because it was now time to bring more balance to my preaching.

Thus, I came back from that retreat with a mandate from the Lord that I then shared with the staff. I said, "We *must* equip every member for ministry. They have to know what their gifts are and how they can be used, and then be deployed—not only within the church but out there in the lost and spiritually hungry world. This is where we must focus in the coming year."

This kind of balanced preaching and teaching represents the second element of Jethro's three-part prescription for Moses's dysfunctional pastorate. Here's the third.

3. RAISE UP LEADERS

After advising Moses to devote himself to prayer and ministering the Word, Jethro added this:

> Moreover you shall select from all the people able men, such as fear
> God, men of truth, hating covetousness; and place such over them to
> be rulers of thousands, rulers of hundreds, rulers of fifties, and rulers
> of tens. (Exodus 18:21)

To paraphrase Jethro, the third item on your job description is to *raise up leaders.* Here's a Bible question for you. Isn't there a New Testament incident that parallels this event in Moses's life to a certain extent? Isn't there a scenario in the book of Acts in which these same three activities are highlighted? Take a look at this passage:

> Now in those days, when the number of the disciples was multiplying,
> there arose a complaint against the Hebrews by the Hellenists, because
> their widows were neglected in the daily distribution. Then the twelve
> summoned the multitude of the disciples and said, "It is not desirable
> that we should leave the word of God and serve tables. Therefore, breth-
> ren, seek out from among you seven men of good reputation, full of the
> Holy Spirit and wisdom, whom we may appoint over this business; but
> we will give ourselves continually to prayer and to the ministry of the
> word." (Acts 6:1–4)

Here we have not one, but a whole group of pastors, overwhelmed and on the verge of burnout. This time it's the twelve apostles swamped by the challenge of managing all the logistics and ministry needs that come with explosive growth. The brand-new church founded by the resurrected Jesus was growing so fast, that administrative tasks—such as making sure all of the widows being looked after by the First Christian Church of Jerusalem got proper care—were being neglected.

Notice how the apostles reacted after they received the complaint: "We're not going to get directly involved in administrating the church's Meals on Chariot Wheels Program because it is best for everyone if we give ourselves to prayer and the ministry of the Word. But we'll make sure it gets done!"

In many quarters today the apostles' response would be viewed with horror and condemnation. I can hear it now: "Elitists!" "Heartless!" "Aloof!" "Out of touch!" But the apostles understood something many Christians and their pastors today do not. Namely, that a pastor's highest and most crucial responsibility is to devote himself to the Word and to prayer. It is for the sake of the physical, emotional, and spiritual well-being of every member that the pastor must resist the demands to be involved in every aspect of administration and ministry at the expense of ample time before God and in His Word.

If we as senior pastors can't wait tables *and* spend adequate time in the presence of the Lord, then the table waiting is going to have to be the thing to go. Yet countless pastors today find themselves with little or no time for extended fellowship with God, constantly recycling old sermons or hastily slapping together fresh ones at the last minute precisely because they spend most of their available time and energy waiting on tables.

When the apostles were faced with that dilemma, the Holy Spirit led them to a powerful solution. They raised up leaders. The role of deacon was born.

As with Jethro and Moses, the apostles realized that the key to being able to consistently devote themselves to the first two parts of the pastor's job description (prayer and study/sermon preparation) was the third part—identifying, training, and empowering leaders to whom they could delegate the work of administration and ministry.

You'll notice that I broke that third piece of the job description up into three parts as well. That's no accident. The fact is, your ability to grow in size and impact will live or die upon your success in these areas:

1. Successfully identifying and attracting outstanding leaders to join you in the work
2. Properly cultivating and training those leaders—setting them into their proper place
3. Empowering those leaders—striking the ideal balance between providing accountability and training while avoiding the common sin of micromanaging

We'll explore some keys to these steps in the chapters that follow.

19

The Prayer of the Burned-Out Pastor

AS WE'VE SEEN, JETHRO'S THREE-PART PRESCRIPTION for Moses—a pastor teetering on the edge of burnout—was basically pray, stay in the Word, and duplicate yourself by raising up leaders and delegating responsibility to them.

Jethro, being a good consultant, didn't just throw out some general advice, hand him an invoice, then walk away. Instead he gave Moses very specific, actionable steps to take. He said, "Moreover you shall select from all the people able men, such as fear God, men of truth, hating covetousness; and place such over them to be rulers of thousands, rulers of hundreds, rulers of fifties, and rulers of tens" (Exodus 18:21).

Let me make two quick observations about this advice before we see how it was implemented.

First, please notice that Jethro advised Moses to look for three things in people before choosing them for leadership. He said select "able" men. Ability matters. Talent, skill, and experience are not irrelevant when it comes to choosing those who will help you carry the load. But ability isn't the *only* thing to look for. He went on specify that these men "fear God," referring to their spiritual condition and the quality of their relationship with the Lord. Finally, he suggested that the candidates should be honest and free from envy—in other words, have strong character.

Jethro's advice was essentially, *Moses, you're looking for a blend of ability, spiritual depth, and character.* He went on to suggest that once such leaders were identified, "place such over them to be rulers of thousands, rulers of hundreds, rulers of fifties, and rulers of tens." Put another way, Jethro recommended a multilayered management structure.

I've noticed that a lot of emerging leaders today seem to be afraid of hierarchy and levels of management. Many have been taught to view the pyramid-style organization as an unhip, overly rigid relic of the past. Others view a top-down management structure as too corporate to be spiritual. But what is being suggested here is precisely that.

Now it's certainly possible to have too many layers of management; nevertheless, as your church grows, your staff and volunteer leaders must grow commensurately. One person can lead, train, and provide meaningful accountability to only so many people (as Moses discovered). And as your staff and volunteer pool grows, additional layers of management will be required. Otherwise, you and your associates will all fall prey to burnout—which, in turn, eventually leads to what I call the prayer of the burned-out pastor.

In the book of Numbers we find Moses stressed out, overwhelmed, and overrun with needy people looking to him for practically everything:

> Then Moses heard the people weeping throughout their families, everyone at the door of his tent.... So Moses said to the LORD, "Why have You afflicted Your servant?... [Why have] You...laid the burden of all these people on me?... For they weep all over me, saying, 'Give us meat, that we may eat.'" (11:10–13)

Sound familiar at all? I suspect most pastors will relate to that sense of being crushed by the burdens of leading a congregation. In fact, I recently read that one in three pastors ultimately leaves full-time ministry prematurely. And a much higher percentage admit to seriously considering calling it quits.

Moses too felt that unrelenting weight and prayed for the ultimate change in job description—death by lightning strike:

I can't carry all these people by myself! The load is far too heavy! If this is

how you intend to treat me, just go ahead and kill me. Do me a favor

and spare me this misery! (verses 14–15, NLT)

Or to paraphrase: "Dear Lord, if You like me at all, just kill me. Seriously, God, just kill me here and now."

I have known many a pastor over the years who, when gut-level honest, would admit to having prayed a prayer similar at one time or another (or at least thought it). I'll just go ahead and confess now to having had such a prayer cross my mind in my early days as a pastor.

The burden of being a senior pastor is far greater than most lay people can imagine. As shepherds, we feel the full weight of looking after the spiritual well-being of our flocks. Every report of a marriage in trouble, negative report from the doctor, wayward child, addiction, bondage, or conflict in the membership weighs upon us. Of course, we hear the good reports too. But human nature dictates that we are much more likely to hear the negative ones. It seems that news of criticism, complaints, and crises simply travels on stronger, faster legs.

It's why so many good people who were called by God to pastor a church are selling insurance or teaching history instead. It's why so many ultimately leave the ministry. And it's why those who stay find themselves stretched to the limit.

As we've just seen, we're in good company. The first known person to pray the "Just kill me, God" prayer was none other than the original burned-out pastor—Moses.

Fortunately for all of us, God didn't directly answer Moses's prayer, but rather He provided him with a wise and powerful solution for managing his crucial role. In direct response to Moses's radical cry for help, we find:

So the LORD said to Moses: "Gather to Me seventy men of the elders of

Israel, whom you know to be the elders of the people and officers over

them; bring them to the tabernacle of meeting, that they may stand

there with you." (Numbers 11:16)

Allow me to paraphrase and summarize God's solution for the burned-out senior pastor, Moses. Paralleling Jethro's advice, God Himself commanded, *Raise up leaders!*

Please notice that God's specific command was to gather seventy elders "whom *you know* to be the elders of the people and officers over them." He didn't say gather those whom the *people* consider to be elders. He didn't say hold an election. He didn't suggest a democratic process for determining who was fit to lead. He put that decision directly into the discerning hands of the senior pastor, Moses. Why? Because Moses was the one accountable before God for the well-being of the entire body!

I understand all too well the trap most pastors of growing churches fall into. For most of us, the devil quickly comes to realize he can't get in front of us and block our way. So instead he gets behind us and pushes—selling the lie that we have to do *everything*, do it *personally*, and do it *immediately*.

The Enemy keeps us so busy doing *good* things that we neglect the *vital* things. For the senior pastor, those vital things are, first and always, time with God and study of His Word.

In practical terms, how do you follow God's advice to Moses? I ask myself two questions at least once each year, forcing myself to be brutally honest about the answers: *What am I doing as a pastor that* no one else *can do?* And then, *What am I doing that* someone else can *do?*

The answers reveal the areas which I need to delegate to able leaders and those which I need to concentrate on personally. I then identify able men and women of character and kindred hearts. I empower them. And then I release them to succeed, being diligent not to micromanage or control.

Finally, notice that God told Moses to bring these leaders "to the tabernacle of meeting." Let's look at this passage again, this time with more of God's instruction to provide some context:

So the LORD said to Moses: "Gather to Me seventy men of the elders of Israel, whom you know to be the elders of the people and officers over them; bring them to the tabernacle of meeting, that they may stand there with you. Then I will come down and talk with you there. I will take of the Spirit that is upon you and will put the same upon them; and they shall bear the burden of the people with you, that you may not bear it yourself alone. (Numbers 11:16–17)

God didn't instruct Moses to simply handpick seventy leaders. He advised that once they had been chosen, Moses was to bring them with him as he fellowshipped with the Lord in the tabernacle. Why? According to God's own words, it was so they could partake of the anointing that rested on Moses! Then God explained the objective of the entire exercise: Moses would no longer have to bear the burdens of pastoring alone. "They shall bear the burden of the people with you," the Lord explained.

☙ Keys to a Blessed Church

I'm often asked how I have been able to oversee one of the fastest growing congregations in America without burning out or losing focus. I can assure you, it is not because I'm special. I can also tell you I am never tempted to pray, *Kill me now!*

> So the LORD said to Moses: "Gather to Me seventy men of the elders of Israel, whom you know to be the elders of the people and officers over them; bring them to the tabernacle of meeting, that they may stand there with you." (Numbers 11:16)

God Himself is describing a method of mentoring and equipping leaders—doing so in a way that infuses them with aspects of your unique relationship with Him, gives them vital understanding of your calling, and actually causes them to receive from the Spirit of God supernatural enablement that is harmonious with the one He has given you. That's pretty cool!

That's how you raise up leaders. You bring them into God's presence with you. You let them observe the dynamic of your relationship with Him. Then you begin to give them some responsibility in the tabernacle.

How have I applied this principle in my own ministry? I have learned to make sure my leaders and I meet with God *together*—and regularly. For example, we open every elders' meeting with a time of worship and prayer. (More on this in the "Culture of Worship" chapter.) Our top-tier leaders and I also get away regularly to be in the presence of God together. I've learned that after future leaders have been brought into dynamic small-group worship and prayer, they are never the same again!

I'm often asked how I have been able to oversee one of the fastest growing congregations in America without burning out or losing focus. I can assure you, it is not because I'm special. But I can also tell you I am never tempted to pray, *Kill me now!* Why? It is only because I long ago learned God's answer to the prayer of the burned-out pastor.

But again, it's not enough to identify leaders and give them responsibility. You have to empower them to carry out that responsibility successfully. And as you're about to discover, there are some key spiritual insights that make that kind of success possible.

20

Eagle's Nest Empowerment

As we've seen, there is a New Testament parallel to Jethro's sage advice to Moses. It is the apostles' Holy Spirit–led determination to delegate ministry administration responsibilities so that they could devote themselves to prayer and preaching. So what about God's direct advice to Moses? I'm referring to the command God gave Moses to raise up leaders he could train and to whom he could delegate the work of ministry. Not surprisingly, we find a New Testament parallel for that counsel too.

Throughout the Gospels we find Jesus modeling this advice in the way He handled His disciples. First Jesus brought His followers with Him so they could observe Him doing the work of ministry. Then He performed ministry *with* them. And ultimately, He sent them out two by two to conduct ministry on their own!

You'll recall that God instructed Moses to choose seventy elders through whom he could duplicate himself. These would share the burden of ministry. Do you recall how many Jesus sent out?

After these things the Lord appointed seventy others also, and sent them two by two before His face into every city and place where He Himself was about to go. Then He said to them, "The harvest truly is great, but the laborers are few; therefore pray the Lord of the harvest to send out laborers into His harvest. Go your way; behold, I send you out as lambs among wolves. (Luke 10:1–3)

Jesus sent out seventy others! Moses appointed seventy as well! Isn't that interesting?

First you demonstrate your values and methods of ministry to the leaders you are raising up. Then you have those emerging leaders join you in ministry. Then you release them, empowering them in ministry as you provide a healthy balance of accountability and autonomy.

This is the approach I've tried to emulate in raising up leaders at Gateway Church. I've sometimes called it the Eagle's Nest approach. I have read that when young fledglings grow big enough to learn to fly, the parents will begin gradually forcing them out of the nest. But the young learners are not left to discover the secrets of flight on their own. Early on, an eaglet will be nudged out of the nest (perhaps with a piece of food), and one of the parents will fly beside it in order to demonstrate the keys to flying.

I know eagles don't actually talk, but I can imagine the parents teaching and exhorting their young students as they fly: "Flap harder! Now, do you feel that thermal updraft? Stretch out your wings. Feel that? You can soar!"

Later on, as their confidence grows, the young eagles begin to take a few solo flights without their parents at their sides. Eventually, they are accomplished flyers ready to teach others.

With the eagles as inspiration, my approach to training leaders could be described as "Nudge them out of the nest and fly beside them." I believe in giving them real responsibility, but I don't just leave them to figure it out on their own. I fly beside them in the early stages—modeling my preferred approach to ministry and then offering wisdom, coaching, and help as needed.

Over the years I've noticed that some prospective leaders are eager and impatient to test their wings. But some of the most gifted new leaders I've encountered had to be coaxed out of the nest at first. Only a few had to be shoved.

The key is offering the appropriate balance of empowerment with accountability. This isn't an easy or natural balance to strike for many leaders. In my experience, most leaders—depending upon their natural temperament—

tend to fall into one of the three categories: dominators, abdicators, and delegators.

Dominators are imbalanced on the side of too much control. Their underlings are never entrusted with enough authority to ever learn how to handle responsibility. Dominators micromanage everyone around them. As a result, true leaders never develop or emerge under them.

⤳ Keys to a Blessed Church

My approach to training leaders could be described as "Nudge them out of the nest and fly beside them." I believe in giving them real responsibility, but I don't just leave them to figure it out on their own.

And the things that you have heard from me among many witnesses, commit these to faithful men who will be able to teach others also. (2 Timothy 2:2)

Abdicators tilt heavily toward the opposite end of this spectrum. They hand over responsibility without ever providing the training, mentoring, and modeling that equip others for success. The potential leaders under them are given responsibility but without accountability; they are thrown into the deep end of the pool and told to swim. Many end up drowning.

The healthy path—the one characterized by the motto "Nudge them out of the nest and fly beside them"—is the path of the *Delegator.* Delegating involves offering incrementally larger doses of responsibility along with corresponding measures of accountability and coaching.

This is an approach I have been deliberate and passionate about following as I have led Gateway Church over the years. Today this empowerment mind-set—responsibility with accountability—permeates every part of our organizational culture and extends even to our accounting policies. For example, virtually every individual on our staff has a discretionary budget: a designated quantity of money that can be spent each fiscal quarter without requiring anyone else's prior approval. Each of us can spend from our respective budgets without talking to another soul. That's *empowerment.*

However, any and all of those expenditures will show up on a report from our accounting department. The elders can see how I've chosen to spend my discretionary budget, just as I can see how my assistant has spent hers. That's *accountability.*

At Gateway, empowerment manifests in more ways than just latitude in discretionary spending. I believe it's necessary to cultivate an organizational culture of empowerment. This begins with our attitudes and flows outward to key processes. Empowerment requires investing in people and looking for that investment to produce achievable, measurable results.

How does this work itself out in practical terms? We have developed and deployed a framework across the organization that consists of five key elements.

1. OPPORTUNITY

We are very intentional about creating opportunities for ministry or administrative responsibility that are consistent with each individual's gifts, character, preparation, and experience. Of course, this requires that we help staff members and volunteers identify and understand what gifts—both natural and spiritual—they possess.

To that end we have an associate pastor who is responsible for fostering staff development. Out of that office has come an amazing set of evaluation and self-discovery tools that help our people discover their sweet spot—that point where their natural strengths, spiritual gifts, passions, and calling all intersect.

This enables us to get the right people in the right positions. Then we progressively give them opportunities that stretch and challenge them while mentoring them to succeed. (Nudge them out of the nest, then fly beside them!)

2. Specifically Defined Duties

We have learned that ambiguity, fuzziness, and presumption are the archenemies of achievement. When goals and targets are ambiguous, when responsibilities are fuzzily communicated, or when leaders presume that those they lead will know what they're supposed to do and how to go about it, you have a prescription for inefficiency, aimless wandering, and even organizational paralysis.

That's why for each position in the organization we provide a clearly defined job description with responsibilities in writing. These are crafted carefully and prayerfully to harmonize with the established vision of the church and department. We strive to make it as easy as possible for each member of the team to know what is expected and what success looks like.

3. Training

As we've already seen, Jesus's approach to raising up leaders—just as in Jethro's advice to Moses—involved allowing the future leaders to observe the work being done and being done well. Then they received opportunities to help and participate. Next came opportunities to take the lead as the Teacher stood by observing and coaching. Finally, they were ready to run on their own. That is a comprehensive training program.

At Gateway we work hard to provide that kind of training. In the process, we are intentional about providing training that helps the trainee understand our DNA: the vision and values of the church and the department in which the trainee will be working. We also take pains to explain the related systems and process we have developed over the years.

4. Resources

"More bricks with less straw." That was the punishment inflicted on the captive Israelites by their Egyptian taskmasters. Pharaoh raised the quota of bricks they were commanded to produce but without any of the vital straw necessary to make them.

Every week countless Christian workers face their own version of the same dilemma. They are charged with doing great and ambitious things for the kingdom of God without the resources necessary to get the job done. Of course, their leaders don't do this out of cruelty or spite. Many organizations simply aren't wired to think clearly in terms of adequately resourcing what various jobs require—if they think that way at all.

We do our best to make sure every person in every position has access to the resources necessary to succeed. And if the role grows, we have processes in place that allow us to allocate additional resources accordingly.

And how can we be sure those resources are used wisely and effectively? It is because we also provide oversight.

⌇ Keys to a Blessed Church

Countless Christian workers are charged with doing great and ambitious things for the kingdom of God without the resources necessary to get the job done.

> You shall no longer give the people straw to make brick as before. Let them go and gather straw for themselves. And you shall lay on them the quota of bricks which they made before. (Exodus 5:7–8)

5. OVERSIGHT

This, of course, is the essence of our "Fly beside them" approach to training. But even after the season of training is over, it is still necessary to provide protection, direction, encouragement, constructive feedback, and accountability. To be effective, this kind of oversight must be done in a spirit of servanthood:

But Jesus called them to Himself and said, "You know that the rulers of the Gentiles lord it over them, and those who are great exercise authority over them. Yet it shall not be so among you; but whoever desires to become great among you, let him be your servant." (Matthew 20:25–26)

Allow me to state the obvious: For there to be oversight, there must be an *overseer*. And any one leader can only provide meaningful oversight to a finite number of people. That means, as your organization grows, you are going to have to create a hierarchical structure with multiple layers.

I know that many pastors instinctively resist any approach to doing ministry that smacks of worldly business models. They say, "This is a church, not a cold, soulless corporation." I would suggest that over the years businesses have stumbled upon godly principles through trial and error. It's possible to follow biblical wisdom and not even realize it. If a certain approach is working in the world of business, we should stop and ask ourselves why.

The fact is, God's leaders have been building hierarchical organizations for thousands of years. Remember Jethro's wise solution to Moses's burnout problem? He said, "Select out of all the people able men who fear God, men of truth, those who hate dishonest gain; and you shall place these over them *as leaders of thousands, of hundreds, of fifties and of tens*" (Exodus 18:21, NASB).

He's describing layers of management that could be depicted by a traditional organization chart. That's hierarchy. And when you're leading a nomadic group of several million people in the building of a brand-new society and culture, you need a *lot* of layers of management.

As your church grows, you'll need additional layers of management too. Yes, I know that sounds very corporate. Yes, I know it sounds so much more noble and humble to say, "We're not going to have titles and supervisors and managers around here." But if you maintain that philosophy, your organization will likely either collapse under the weight of growth, or it will never really grow at all.

Opportunity, specifically defined duties, training, resources, and oversight—these are the building blocks of an organizational culture of empowerment. But there is a fundamental spiritual foundation upon which all of this must rest. That's the focus of the next chapter.

21

The Vital Key to Being an Empowering Leader

ON MORE OCCASIONS THAN I CAN COUNT, I have heard positive comments about my empowering approach to running a church. I've had more than a few of our recent hires come to me and say something like, "Robert, this is the most empowering place I've ever worked. Thank you for creating an environment where we're free to use our gifts to the fullest."

I'm always both blessed and humbled by these comments. But I'm mostly just grateful. I appreciate hearing that I'm viewed as a leader who empowers those around me. And that is certainly something I have learned to value over the years. But to be honest, I think in the early years I just stumbled into being an empowering leader because, in my naiveté, it didn't occur to me to approach things any other way.

In other words, allowing others to grow and flourish and shine seemed to come naturally to me. It wasn't my natural instinct to feel threatened by the gifts or successes of the people working under my leadership.

When I've been asked about this aspect of my leadership style in the past, I've never been able to give a solid, spiritual, biblical explanation as to why I tend to approach things this way. And since I haven't been able to offer an explanation, it has been difficult for me to help other leaders to whom this empowering approach doesn't come as naturally.

All that changed recently when, after more than thirty years in ministry and intensive Bible study, I saw something in the Word I'd never noticed before.

It was something that reveals both the key to being an empowering leader and the reason why I'd managed to stumble into it.

Not surprisingly, the truth was hiding in plain sight in John's account of the final hours of the most empowering leader to ever walk the face of the earth. Now, I have read the thirteenth chapter of John with its description of the Last Supper countless times. I have been there at the table with Peter, James, John, Judas, and the rest so many times that I'm always a little surprised not to see my face in da Vinci's famous painting.

I suspect you're as familiar with that scene as I am. If so, you know that Jesus began that extraordinary evening by washing the disciples' feet. What I had never noticed until just recently is the Bible's commentary about what prompted that act of service and humility. Right there in the opening verses of the chapter is an insight into Jesus's frame of mind and state of heart:

> *Jesus, knowing that the Father had given all things into His hands, and that*
> *He had come from God and was going to God,* rose from supper and laid
> aside His garments, took a towel and girded Himself. After that, He
> poured water into a basin and began to wash the disciples' feet, and to
> wipe them with the towel with which He was girded. (John 13:3–5)

Why had I never noticed the first part of verse 3 before? Here is the explanation for the stunning fact that the King of Glory, the Incarnate Word who existed before time itself, bowed down before mere men and washed the filth from their feet. Here was the solution to the mind-blowing mystery of how the Creator could serve the creation.

Jesus could serve and delegate authority with confidence because He knew three things.

1. JESUS KNEW WHERE POWER COMES FROM

Note that John 13:3 says Jesus knew "that the Father had given all things into His hands." In the typical wealthy household of Jesus's day, the designated foot washer was the lowest-ranking servant. When you saw the servant whose job it was to wash feet, you could be confident you were looking at the guy who aspired to getting promoted to shoveling out the barn.

Only people who are secure in who they are and in what they have are fully free to choose the role of the servant. Only people who know beyond all doubt that they have God's approval can cast aside the bondage of seeking people's approval. Only those who are at peace knowing that it is God who has given them what they have and that no mortal can take it away from them are fully free to give away what they have.

This truth reveals the reason a leader will tenaciously cling to authority, influence, and position. It's because in his heart of hearts he's not sure that "God has given all things into his hands." He's operating from the deception that he has gotten his position and authority through his own hard work, striving, and cleverness. And since he thinks he attained it by his own strength, he assumes he must hang onto it the same way.

Another leader may be operating from a deep root of insecurity. He may secretly believe that someone more gifted, more charismatic, or more educated may come along at any moment and take what is his. He secretly believes that at any moment the affection and esteem of others, the prestige he enjoys, and the influence he wields may be siphoned away by another. So he maintains a white-knuckle grip on what he has. He dares not allow anyone he leads to fly too high or shine too brightly.

This house of fear and insecurity is built upon a false foundation. The key to being an empowering leader is simply knowing where power comes from:

> For exaltation [promotion] comes neither from the east
> Nor from the west nor from the south.
> But God is the Judge:
> He puts down one,
> And exalts another. (Psalm 75:6–7)

These things says He who is holy, He who is true, "He who has the key
of David, He who opens and no one shuts, and shuts and no one opens":
"I know your works. See, I have set before you an open door, and no one
can shut it." (Revelation 3:7–8)

When some of John the Baptist's disciples started getting alarmed about
Jesus's growing fame and following, John shut them down quickly, asserting the
fact that "a man can receive nothing unless it has been given to him from heaven"
(John 3:27).

John knew where power comes from. He recognized that whatever we have
is on loan from God and that whatever we are given is to be held with an open
hand before Him.

This revelation helped me understand why empowering others has seemed
to come a little more naturally for me than for others. It is because I learned early
on in my Christian walk to hold what God has given me with an open hand. I
learned it first with money. Later I learned it extended to everything else in my
life—including my position and authority.

Don't get me wrong! There are countless aspects of the Christian life and
spiritual leadership that took God years to get into my thick skull. But this one
thing was a miraculous work God did in my heart very early in my Christian
walk. And that work was deep, comprehensive, and profound. Now that I think
about it, it makes sense. Once God has led you to give away numerous cars, a
house, and, on more than one occasion, your entire life savings—and in each
case you've seen God unfailingly restore and bless you abundantly in response—
trusting Him as you give away your ministry comes much easier.

This stems from and fosters an abundance mentality. It's the quiet confidence that God has plenty, and that if He asks you to give away what you have,
He is faithful and just to restore you. You know there's much more where that
came from.

The opposite is a scarcity mentality. It is the false belief that any resource—

money, love, esteem, influence, opportunity—is limited. This paradigm also assumes that power comes from a place other than God—from ourselves, from random chance, from a system, or from denominational headquarters. If in your heart you believe these things, you will not hold what you've been given with an open hand.

✑ Keys to a Blessed Church

> An abundance mentality is the quiet confidence that God has plenty, and that if He asks you to give what you have away, He is faithful and just to restore you.
>
> > Then Jesus, looking at him, loved him, and said to him, "One thing you lack: Go your way, sell whatever you have and give to the poor, and you will have treasure in heaven; and come, take up the cross, and follow Me." (Mark 10:21)

Not long ago I heard a fellow pastor talk about his experience of being a foster parent for an orphaned child. A six-year-old little boy had lived in a desperately poor, dysfunctional home with a drug-addicted single mother. She had consistently spent all available money on drugs, so he had known little but hunger and lack. Eventually she died of a drug overdose and didn't return home. He lived alone for weeks before someone noticed him and called Child Protective Services.

The pastor and his wife had been called to see if they would be foster parents for the boy for a season, and they happily agreed.

In the boy's first days in their home, the pastor noticed the boy routinely stuffing food from the dinner table into his pockets. He came to realize that the boy had never known abundance. Scarcity and unpredictability were all he had ever experienced. He grabbed food while it was available because he had no reason to expect that there would be any more food in the future.

It took the boy several weeks of living in this home before he began to realize that those caring for him had plenty and could be relied upon. Eventually he stopped hoarding food. He shifted from a scarcity mind-set to one of abundance. (Please don't be turned off by my use of the word *abundance* simply because some have used it with a selfish motive.)

Sadly, many pastors and leaders are operating with a scarcity mind-set. They can't bring themselves to openly share authority, credit, or rewards, because they aren't convinced there is plenty to go around. In other words, they don't know where power comes from.

On more than one occasion I've been surprised to observe a pastor who will readily and confidently teach the principle of sowing and reaping when it comes to finances—that is, God is faithful to bless you with more when you give with a right heart—and yet that same pastor is too fearful to give power and authority away because he doesn't trust God to bless him with more.

2. JESUS KNEW WHERE HE CAME FROM

Jesus served His followers and gave them authority because He knew "the Father had given all things into His hands." But as John 13:3 says, that's not all He knew. Look at that verse again: "Jesus, knowing that the Father had given all things into His hands, and that He had come from God and was going to God."

Jesus knew that He had come from God. You're probably, thinking, *Well, of course Jesus came from God. He was His only begotten Son.* Yes, but you and I come from God too if we have been born again. We were lost and dead in our sins, but in Christ we have been born of God.

Whoever believes that Jesus is the Christ is born of God, and everyone
who loves Him who begot also loves him who is begotten of Him.
(1 John 5:1)

I know where I came from. Knowing this makes all the difference in the world for me as a leader. Remembering how lost, wretched, clueless, and self-destructive I was *without* Christ—and how forgiven, whole, accepted, and empowered I am *in* Christ—helps me stay in thankful dependence upon Him. And it gives me the confidence to serve others because only He could redeem a mess like me.

As leaders, it's vital that we know where we came from. It guards our footsteps from stumbling through pride, and it prevents us from falling prey to the presumption that we can do anything in our own power.

3. JESUS KNEW WHERE HE WAS GOING

Jesus stripped to the waist and bowed down before His followers to serve them like a slave because He knew He "was going to God." In other words, He had a clear, compelling vision of His future and the rewards He would enjoy there.

Does it startle you to think that Jesus needed to focus on future blessings in order to summon the courage to endure the unspeakable hardships of the Cross? That's precisely what the writer of Hebrews tells us:

> [Look] unto Jesus, the author and finisher of our faith, who for the
> joy that was set before Him endured the cross, despising the shame,
> and has sat down at the right hand of the throne of God. (Hebrews
> 12:2)

If a clear and compelling vision of future joy was necessary for the Son of God to fulfill His mission as a leader, how much more vital is it for you and me? We have to know where we're going and that where we're going is good.

Yes, if we're going to be empowering leaders, it's crucial to know that everything we have has come from the hand of a loving, trustworthy God of abundance. And it's vital to know where we came from, what we've been redeemed out of, and that our new birth gives us a new heritage. But we must also know where we are going. We have to know that God rewards faithfulness and obedience.

We have to be confident that joy lies ahead if we will submit to serving and empowering those whom He has entrusted to our leadership.

Holding all God has given you with an open hand... This is the little-known key to being an empowering leader. And teaching those around you to do the same will help you build a culture of empowerment in your church or organization.

 PART 5

Blessed Government

22

Church Government Matters

LET'S CALL THIS A TALE OF TWO TYPES OF CHURCHES. One pastor, but two church types. I'll call this pastor John. John is a man who grew up within one of America's established denominations where he heard and answered a call of God to preach; he attended one of that denomination's seminaries after college.

A naturally gifted communicator with a winning way about him, John experienced immediate success as a young pastor. He was a fountain of fresh ideas and visionary energy, and after a short stay in his first job out of seminary, a search committee from a large, long-established church in a bigger city sought him out.

John leapt at the opportunity. It seemed he had arrived, and he was looking forward to exercising his leadership and vision casting in an influential congregation. This is Church 1 in our tale of two churches.

Shortly after arriving, John was shocked to discover that instead of becoming *the* dynamic leader, he would not be in charge in any meaningful way. The deacon/elder board consisted of older men who had been in place for decades. This body made all key decisions regarding the church. The pastor was free to offer ideas for initiatives and projects, but the board alone held the power to decide what would get done. In other words, John could propose, but the board could dispose.

Of course, these elders had seen many pastors come and go over those years. All of these they had recruited and hired, just as they had with John. Some of

John's predecessors had moved on to other opportunities. A few had retired. And one had even been fired by this governing board. When John asked about this particular incident, the board said something about this former pastor failing to adequately carry out core duties of the job, such as hospital visitation and calling on the homebound elderly.

But John knew that several objective observers suggested that it was really more about a clash of wills and visions. The pastor at that time had wanted to make the primary weekend worship services more contemporary and progressive to attract younger families to the predominantly silver-haired congregation. The board would have none of it. They and the pastor butted heads until the board finally decided the strong-willed preacher had to go.

All of this eventually led John to a troubling conclusion. Namely, in the system in which he operated, he was actually just a key employee of an organization—an employee who had been hired to perform a certain set of tasks. Those tasks were: to preach at a level that kept people coming to church and excited about giving, to visit the sick and elderly, and to perform weddings and funerals.

His constant and escalating clashes with the governing board fueled a growing sense of frustration in John. (You will recall my reference to holy discontent in chapter 7.) Furthermore, he was increasingly haunted by Jesus's discourse about shepherds in the gospel of John. There the Lord contrasted the true shepherd with the hireling.

> I am the good shepherd. The good shepherd gives His life for the sheep.
> But a hireling, he who is not the shepherd, one who does not own the
> sheep, sees the wolf coming and leaves the sheep and flees; and the wolf
> catches the sheep and scatters them. The hireling flees because he is a
> hireling and does not care about the sheep. (10:11–13)

John knew he did not have the heart of a hireling beating within his chest. He loved the sheep. He was, he believed, ready and willing to lay down his life for the sheep. Indeed, that was why he was so frustrated by being stymied by the elder board at every turn. He was being treated as a hireling whether he was one or not, because the church's very system of government *made* him a hireling.

After several years of this deteriorating situation, he'd had enough. He began to make plans to step out and found a church of his own nearby—separate and independent from the denomination he'd known all his life. He had no substantial disagreements with the denomination on doctrine. He was simply unwilling to pastor within the system of church government that the denomination required of all its affiliates.

In his pain and frustration, John made a fierce inner vow. *When I have my own church, never again will a group of stubborn, ancient, close-minded naysayers and sticks-in-the-mud control my ability to lead and carry out my vision.*

When the time was right, he resigned and launched his new work in a high school cafeteria. And he was true to that vow. He established "his" church as a nonprofit corporation and filled the legally required complement of board members with his wife, a close pastor friend, and some admirers who were successful businessmen.

John's days of battling and politicking to advance his vision were over. Not a single voice on the board was likely to do anything but heartily endorse whatever John planned to do. He was finally in control. This is Church 2 in our tale of two churches.

This new work grew rapidly, as John knew it would. And in the early years of that growth, John was living a dream come true. He was essentially able to create a church in his own image. The programs, initiatives, and spending priorities were whatever John decided they should be. Of course, John did his best to follow the Lord's leading and direction for the church. But if he felt that he'd heard from heaven, he didn't feel the need to check or confirm that direction with anyone else. Of course, the rapidly growing staff wasn't inclined to challenge him on anything. And to the degree there was discussion in staff meetings, it ended the moment John played the "God told me" card.

The board met once a year as the laws governing nonprofits require. These meetings were casual, friendly times of fellowship, with only a few minutes spent "moving" and "seconding" in order to accept the minutes of the previous year's meeting and to approve the current year's financial report. Between these meetings, John would occasionally call one of the board members to seek his advice on a matter. He would weigh that advice and then proceed as he thought best.

This arrangement seemed to work beautifully in the early years of the church's life. But as the fellowship grew, so did the budgets. The organization's needs became more sophisticated; problems became exponentially more complex; the stakes soared; and the negative implications of a bad decision grew increasingly punishing.

Eventually, even with the best of intentions, John led the church down a disastrous path. Initially, some people around him had meekly questioned the wisdom of the endeavor. But in the end, there really wasn't anyone in John's ministry life with the position and posture to challenge him in any meaningful way.

The resulting fallout caused a large exodus from the church and damage to the church's reputation in the community.

Before you start trying to figure out who John *really* is, you need to know that he is actually a composite of many pastors I have encountered over the years. This composite neatly illustrates a truth I want to convey. Namely, that the vast majority of pastors today are functioning out of balance where authority and accountability—the elements and products of church government—are concerned. In other words, most forms of church government are in one ditch or the other. John's not-uncommon story reveals how it's possible to go from one extreme to the other.

Church government isn't a glamorous topic, but it is a vital one. The form of government a church adopts matters more than most people ever dream. So in the remaining chapters in this section, we'll explore the balanced approach the Bible prescribes and that God blesses.

ஜ Keys to a Blessed Church

The majority of pastors are functioning out of balance where authority and accountability are concerned. Most forms of church government are in one ditch or the other.

> Likewise you younger people, submit yourselves to your elders. Yes, all of you be submissive to one another, and be clothed with humility, for "God resists the proud, But gives grace to the humble." (1 Peter 5:5)

23

The Gateway Approach to Church Government

A SINGLE KEY ASSUMPTION SERVES AS THE FOUNDATION for Gateway's approach to church government: The church is the hope of the world.

As the body of Christ, the church is the visible, tangible manifestation of Jesus in the earth today. The Scarlet Thread of Redemption that began in a promise to Eve—that her seed would one day crush the head of the serpent—ran through Abraham's founding of a nation, through the first Passover, through the Law and the prophets, culminated in the cross of Jesus Christ, and now leads to His church. We are God's agents of redemption and restoration on earth. We are walking out the implications of Jesus's victory over death and the curse. However...

In order for the church to have the maximum impact in this world, it must have a healthy governing structure. When a church chooses its government—whether it realizes it or not—it molds, shapes, and casts its destiny.

Why is this so? It is because church government is the channel through which vision flows—from God to leaders, then on to His people. And it is the context in which kingdom destiny is expressed for the individuals serving in His work.

Our view of church government has two additional foundational concepts:

1. Theocratic Rule
2. Plural Leadership with Singular Headship

Whatever style or structure of government is in place must reflect these two important bedrock concepts. Allow me to explain the terms and how they inform our approach to church government.

✒ Keys to a Blessed Church

> No church is going to be better than its government. When a church chooses its government—whether it realizes it or not—it molds, shapes, and casts its destiny.

> Let the elders who rule well be counted worthy of double honor, especially those who labor in the word and doctrine. (1 Timothy 5:17)

THEOCRATIC RULE

At the heart of our approach to government is a seemingly obvious but often overlooked assumption: God is in charge and Jesus is King.

As Psalm 24:1 puts it, "The earth is the LORD's, and all its fullness." All rightful authority and power on the earth belongs to God, and only He can grant it to others. This is the essence of Romans 13:1–2:

> Everyone must submit himself to the governing authorities, for there is no authority except that which God has established. The authorities that exist have been established by God. Consequently, he who rebels against the authority is rebelling against what God has instituted, and those who do so will bring judgment on themselves. (NIV)

If, as the Word declares here, *all* earthly authority is God established, this must be doubly true of authority in the church. That means a biblical approach to church government must be based on the concept that all leaders must function as representatives for God and His kingdom.

This paradigm obviously demands that church government be taken seriously by everyone involved. Leaders who embrace this understanding will be super-diligent to advance the interests of God's kingdom rather than their own selfish interests or careers. And church members will understand that since all authority derives from God, when they obey that authority they are, by faith, obeying God.

There is a second key presupposition behind our approach to church government.

SINGULAR HEADSHIP AND PLURAL LEADERSHIP

The previous chapter presented the parable of a pastor named John in two different church government scenarios. In the first instance, John found himself at a church governed solely by plural leadership—an elder board that hired and fired the pastor as they saw fit and made all the key decisions in the church. In the second scenario, we saw John overreacting to the abuses and unhealthy constraints of his first pastorate by jumping into the ditch on the other side of the road. Basically, he created for himself a singular headship government situation. My friend Jimmy Evans calls the first extreme a shepherd-beating government and the other extreme a sheep-beating government!

Neither arrangement is healthy. And neither, in my view, conforms to the biblical ideal. What is the ideal? You won't be surprised that it's a balanced blend of the two extremes. This is the approach to government we did our best to build into Gateway Church from Day One. Our execution hasn't always been perfect. We may have veered from the center of the path a little from time to time. But because our hearts' cry has been to do things God's way, He has consistently been faithful to bring us back to balanced order.

What is the biblical case for singular headship–plural leadership model of church government? Here are two examples, one from the New Testament and one from the Old (which we examined in part 4):

The reason I left you in Crete was that you might straighten out what was left unfinished and appoint elders in every town, as I directed you. (Titus 1:5, NIV)

Moses' father-in-law replied, "What you are doing is not good. You and these people who come to you will only wear yourselves out. The work is too heavy for you; you cannot handle it alone. Listen now to me and I will give you some advice, and may God be with you. You must be the people's representative before God and bring their disputes to him. Teach them the decrees and laws, and show them the way to live and the duties they are to perform. But select capable men from all the people—men who fear God, trustworthy men who hate dishonest gain—and appoint them as officials over thousands, hundreds, fifties and tens. Have them serve as judges for the people at all times, but have them bring every difficult case to you; the simple cases they can decide themselves. That will make your load lighter, because they will share it with you. If you do this and God so commands, you will be able to stand the strain, and all these people will go home satisfied." (Exodus 18:17–23, NIV)

In each instance God uses a singular head to establish the vision, values, and direction of the work, *together with* a plurality, or group of people, to walk out the vision, monitor and report results, and participate in fleshing out the fullness of the vision.

As we've already observed, balance between these two elements in church government is exceedingly rare. In fact, if you visualize the relationship between these two elements as a seesaw, in many cases one end of the teetertotter is institutionally bolted to the ground.

In some cases, the bylaws of the church or the denominational structure has the side on which the elder/deacon board sits firmly anchored to terra firma, leaving the near-powerless pastor high up in the air with his legs dangling and flailing in a futile effort to reach the ground. Other structures are meticulously designed to so heavily weight the side of the founder/pastor that two dozen frantic elders can't budge it upward an inch.

Of course, an infinite number of variations can be found between these two extremes. But again, balance is hard to find among local churches today. And that lack of balanced government tends to stifle their effectiveness or leave them open to destructive forces. I've seen it time and again. Generally, this imbalance manifests itself in one of two extremes:

1. spiritual domination by one man

2. political control by a group

This imbalance exacts a steep price from the church. Payment usually comes in the form of debilitating internal tension, mistrust, and invariably, a failure to achieve the vital goals of ministry. And I don't need to remind you that the eternal destinies of millions hinge on our ability to carry out our respective missions with power and effectiveness.

On the other hand, the rewards of balanced leadership are great. The fruits of a biblical balance of authority in the local church include internal peace, trust, and, most importantly, the power to excel at accomplishing God's will and kingdom work.

Of course, all of this raises some key questions, which you may be asking right now: How is that kind of balance achieved and maintained? Is it even possible to implement a balanced approach within a denominational hierarchy? And what does the singular headship–plural leadership approach look like in practice?

Fear not. In the chapters that follow I will offer answers to all these questions and more. And I will provide some real-world examples of how these concepts work themselves out in the daily life of our church government processes.

24

Healthy Tension

I BELIEVE ONE OF THE MOST SIGNIFICANT FACTORS contributing to Gateway's health is our ability to maintain an appropriate balance—a healthy tension if you will—between my singular headship as a pastor and the plural leadership of our elders and senior staff.

I'm not boasting. I'm simply pointing out that we have been very prayerful and intentional about this. We have adopted a paradigm that heads off classic church power struggles before they start by acknowledging a vital truth: Power doesn't lie in the office of pastor. Nor does it lie in the office of elder. Power in the church lies with Jesus:

> And He is the head of the body, the church, who is the beginning, the firstborn from the dead, that in all things He may have the preeminence. (Colossians 1:18)

> And He put all things under His feet, and gave Him to be head over all things to the church, which is His body, the fullness of Him who fills all in all. (Ephesians 1:22–23)

The power struggles that are all too common in churches are an affront to the God who offered His Son as a sacrifice to redeem us all. They are born of the same insecure spirit of striving and self-promotion that prompted James and John (prior to their salvation) to ask Jesus for the right to sit at the right and left of His throne in the kingdom (see Mark 10:35–37).

✑ Keys to a Blessed Church

Acknowledging this vital truth tends to head off classic church power struggles before they can begin: Power doesn't lie in the office of pastor or in the office of elder. Power in the church lies with Jesus.

> All things were created through Him and for Him.
> And He is before all things, and in Him all things
> consist. And He is the head of the body, the church,
> who is the beginning, the firstborn from the dead,
> that in all things He may have the preeminence.
> (Colossians 1:16–18)

Where does power lie? As we've already noted, it lies with God. He has, however, delegated *responsibility* and *authority* to pastors and elders. How does this work itself out at Gateway?

We view the pastor as one member of the elder body—a special member. In other words, the pastor is chief among equals. But what is vital to making the relationship work is that everyone involved approaches the role in a spirit of humility and mutual submission. At Gateway, the elders submit to me individually as the pastor, and I submit to the elders corporately. (You'll see how that works in practice as I unpack these concepts going forward.)

There is another key aspect of our pastor-elder dynamic that is somewhat unorthodox. Most American churches function like a democracy. That is, the majority rules. In most elder-deacon boards, if an idea or project can gather 50 percent support plus one vote, it's going to go forward. But we determined early on that we would move in unity or we wouldn't move at all. In other words, all proposals require a unanimous vote to pass.

Do you mean to tell me, Robert, you may be thinking, *that one reluctant elder can hold up an initiative that you and every other member of the elder board believe is a brilliant, God-ordained idea?*

Yes, that is precisely what I'm telling you. I trust the Spirit of God that resides in each man in the room. If I didn't know them to be mature believers who treasure God's Word and know how to hear His voice, they wouldn't have been selected to be elders. (I'll share more about that process in the chapter titled "Healthy Spiritual Elders.") If we're not in full agreement about something, we take that as a sign that we need to keep praying and seeking God. Perhaps it's the right move, but the timing isn't right. Or maybe God has something better for us around the bend.

As the singular head, I'm not passive about the direction of the church. I lead. But I'm also fully prepared to submit if the elder board isn't in unified agreement about what I have proposed.

This means I go into our elder meetings believing in good faith that I have heard from the Lord about our direction, values, and initiatives. I say clearly and unapologetically, "I believe God has spoken this." But I also have to be equally willing to hold that belief with an open hand. I can't walk into our meeting with a posture that basically suggests, "Guys, I think God wants us to do xyz, but I'll relinquish the idea if you can find a way to pry it out of my white-knuckled grip." And I certainly can't suggest that because I believe I've heard from the Lord that there is no room for discussion or alternative viewpoints.

Open-handed leadership walks into that elders' meeting and says, "Guys, I think I've heard from the Lord about this, but let's pray together and talk. Let's see if you concur." Or maybe we decide I have indeed heard from the Lord but not about the timing. Or perhaps the scope of what the Lord wants is actually broader or narrower than I've assumed. Our overarching approach can be summed up quite simply: "Let's come together and seek the Lord in unity."

In that scenario, I'm leading but I'm not dominating. And if I'm approaching it with the right heart, I will submit to the group if we're not in complete harmony.

"Has that ever happened at Gateway, Robert?" you ask.

Absolutely. It's rare, but there have been several instances in our history when I have deferred or yielded to the group because one or more of the members had sincere concerns about a plan of action. And the fact is, each of the other members of the elder board has occasionally not viewed an issue precisely the way the rest of the group seemed to see it. However, the fact that we only move when we are in unanimous agreement makes us all very sober and thoughtful about using our functional veto. For that reason it's not unheard of to have a situation in which one member has reservations about a matter on which the rest of the group is in agreement, but unless he feels very strongly about it, he'll yield to the balance of the elder board. But each man knows that he is expected to speak up and share his heart—even if it seems to be contrary to what everyone else thinks.

These instances are rare because we're diligent to pray and worship together as a group. The norm is for us to all be on the same page spiritually. But all this is only possible in an atmosphere of trust in each other, mutual respect for the offices of pastor and elder, and humility before God.

That's the secret of healthy tension. Now on to some practical implications of this approach.

25

A Healthy Pastor

OVER THE YEARS WE AT GATEWAY CHURCH HAVE SPENT an amazing amount of time discussing, thinking about, praying about, and seeking God's wisdom concerning church government and healthy structure. On the pages that follow I hope to share some of our collective wisdom and insights on these subjects. Of course, we haven't arrived. We're learning new things every week.

Nevertheless, we believe there are two elements that must be present if a church is going to operate in a healthy state of balance between singular headship and plural leadership. The first of these is obvious: you have to have the right kind of senior pastor.

Of course, that presents the question of how to define *right*. The fact is, God calls a wide variety of personalities and temperaments to the office of pastor. Great pastors come from all types of backgrounds. But within this diversity, I've noticed important common traits among those who excel in this office.

For one thing, a truly exceptional pastor will be a visionary. Nothing is more vital than the ability to receive, communicate, and successfully implement God's vision for the church. And although vision is ultimately carried and implemented through a broad base of ministry leaders—both volunteer and paid—it must begin with the senior pastor.

I believe, with rare exceptions, that vision is *received* by a person and confirmed and clarified by a *group*. This is certainly the pattern we see in Scripture. God grabs Moses's attention through a burning bush, then sends him to the Israelites to tell of His plan. The Lord communicates a plan of attack to Joshua, who then shares with the elders of Israel the seemingly crazy idea of marching around the city of Jericho for several days. The Holy Spirit communicates with Peter in a dream that the gospel is for the Gentiles too, then Peter carries that revelation to the rest of the apostles and on to the church at large. And so it is today.

⤳ Keys to a Blessed Church

> Vision is received by a *person*. It is confirmed and clarified by a *group*. This is the pattern we see in Scripture. The senior pastor must be the chief visionary.
>
> Moreover God said to Moses, "Thus you shall say to the children of Israel." (Exodus 3:15)

Visionaries aren't infallible, however. We're not immune to confusing our own priorities, plans, and preferences with what the Lord is actually saying. That's why another trait that is vital in a senior pastor is what I described earlier as holding his vision with an open hand.

To that end, the pastor must view the eldership as God's voice of confirmation and direction to him. When a pastor begins to view the elders as a jury to be persuaded through his charm and oratorical skills, or as an adversary that must be defeated through crafty strategy or sheer force of will, a breakdown of authority and progress will invariably result.

The pastor is responsible before God to deliver to the eldership what he believes is the heart of God regarding the direction of the church. He is to communicate clearly and plainly what seems right, biblical, and timely to him. Then, holding what he has spoken with an open hand, he should consider the outcome of the elder's discussion and input to God's will.

But Robert, you may be thinking, *what if the elders are wrong?*

Trust God. Rest in the knowledge He is big enough to correct them. (When we turn our attention to the qualifications and characteristics of great elders in the next chapter, we'll see they must be aware they will be accountable to God for their participation with the senior pastor in hearing and following Him.) This is part of the beauty of operating in a system in which the senior pastor and elders must be in unanimity on all decisions. It is a very sobering thing to know that you, as an individual, have the power to keep a kingdom initiative from moving forward.

Leadership ability is another vital trait a senior pastor must possess if a healthy balance is to be maintained. Through preaching, teaching, and communicating, the senior pastor must be able to instruct, inspire, and motivate the congregation to accept and respond to God's will and vision for themselves and the church.

Finally, no church government can function in healthy balance if the senior pastor is not a person of tremendous personal integrity. Of course, he must be a good example to the congregation, staff, and eldership. But as I've noted previously, it's even more vital that he operate in high moral excellence in his personal life. His marriage, family, attitudes, habits, interpersonal skills, spiritual life, and work ethic are all important elements of the platform of authority on which the senior pastor stands.

26

Healthy Spiritual Elders

IN THE PREVIOUS CHAPTER I MENTIONED TWO ELEMENTS that must be in place if a healthy governmental balance of authority and responsibility is going to be maintained. The first is a healthy senior pastor. Since we've explored the traits and qualities in a pastor that make the concept of singular headship with plural leadership work effectively, now we'll examine the second of these elements: a healthy elder body.

You won't be surprised to learn that we've given just as much thought and study to what makes for an outstanding member of an elder body as we have what makes an excellent pastor. Bill Hybels, in his book *Courageous Leadership*, sums it up best with three words: *character, chemistry,* and *competence.* Allow me to elaborate.

CHARACTER

The Bible doesn't leave us guessing about what qualities an elder should possess. For those who wish to be considered for the position of elder at Gateway, they must exhibit the biblical character of an elder:

> This is a faithful saying: If a man desires the position of a bishop, he de-
> sires a good work. A bishop then must be blameless, the husband of one
> wife, temperate, sober-minded, of good behavior, hospitable, able to
> teach; not given to wine, not violent, not greedy for money, but gentle,
> not quarrelsome, not covetous; one who rules his own house well, having

his children in submission with all reverence (for if a man does not know how to rule his own house, how will he take care of the church of God?); not a novice, lest being puffed up with pride he fall into the same condemnation as the devil. Moreover he must have a good testimony among those who are outside, lest he fall into reproach and the snare of the devil. (1 Timothy 3:1–7)

Appoint elders in every city as I commanded you—if a man is blameless, the husband of one wife, having faithful children not accused of dissipation or insubordination. For a bishop must be blameless, as a steward of God, not self-willed, not quick-tempered, not given to wine, not violent, not greedy for money, but hospitable, a lover of what is good, soberminded, just, holy, self-controlled, holding fast the faithful word as he has been taught, that he may be able, by sound doctrine, both to exhort and convict those who contradict. (Titus 1:5–9)

CHEMISTRY

At Gateway, elder business is conducted with the highest value being placed upon unity. Unity, however, is not the same thing as conformity. Meaningful biblical unity provides a safe place for open expressions of sincerely held opinion. The atmosphere should encourage a diversity of viewpoints. An elder board filled with yes men who are inclined to simply go along to get along cannot hold up their end of the delicate singular headship–plural leadership balance.

True and lasting unity comes from valuing relationship above corporate accomplishment, personal fulfillment, or mere policy preferences. We have a saying on the elder board at Gateway that encapsulates this truth: "Relationships above issues."

We believe that when we live in unity, we position ourselves for God's blessing. In fact, that's precisely what is affirmed in Psalm 133:1: "Behold how good and pleasant it is for brethren to dwell together in unity!" It's no accident that the final verse of that short psalm declares, "For there the LORD commanded the blessing—life forevermore" (verse 3).

Unity is paramount. Of course, this is not exactly a revolutionary concept. Many elder boards and deacon bodies value unity and strive for harmony. But there is something about our approach that I believe is rare. That is, our objective is not to come into unity by finding ways to agree with *each other*. The goal is for each of us to come into agreement with *God*. When we all hear clearly and accurately what the Spirit of God is saying, unity is the natural result.

It's very possible for a group of people to be in agreement with each other and yet miss God's will by a mile. We can all be wrong together! Unity around something that runs contrary to what God is saying will not take us very far. That's why the goal of eldership is to come into unity with the Holy Spirit and with what He is saying.

❧ Keys to a Blessed Church

True and lasting unity comes from valuing relationship above corporate accomplishment, personal fulfillment, and mere policy preferences. Remember: "Relationships above issues."

> Now the multitude of those who believed were of one heart and one soul; neither did anyone say that any of the things he possessed was his own, but they had all things in common. (Acts 4:32)

COMPETENCE

The third thing we look for in elder candidates is a certain set of competencies. First and foremost we want to see that the individual is what we call governmentally gifted.

A person gifted in this way will actually tend to derive joy and a sense of satisfaction in the process of overseeing an enterprise, which is precisely why some of our non-staff elders are owners of successful businesses. A person gifted in this way will also have a knack for seeing the whole, rather than becoming fixated on one or two areas of ministry. He will understand and respect the authority structure we have in place and be willing to work within it. We look for men who are secure in themselves and in who they are in the Lord. Why? Because an elder needs to be able to take heat over major decisions without changing his mind or becoming ungracious under pressure. He must be able to defend a position without being intimidated or threatened by opposition.

Finally, we look for an individual who has a loyal heart; in helping to lead the church, he will reflect support for the senior pastor and eldership publicly and to congregation members. Let me repeat, valuing the quality of loyalty is not to be confused with seeking people who will rubber stamp whatever it is the pastor proposes. It is just that an elder must be able to defend the decisions of the group and be able to address disagreements in a godly way.

While conducting the business of the church, an elder must have the temperament in meetings to honestly express disagreements and represent his opinions truthfully and lovingly. However, an adversarial spirit on his part cannot be tolerated.

SHUNNING THE POISON OF POLITICS

Few things are more poisonous to the kind of unity and balance we strive for in our church government than what I call a political spirit.

I'm not referring to politics in the sense of Republican versus Democrat or conservative policy preferences versus liberal ones. I'm talking about a host of attitudes and practices that come with trying to win members of a governing body over to a certain point of view. Campaigning, lobbying, arm twisting, horse trading, and mutual back scratching are all familiar activities to anyone who has tried to get things done in a majority-ruled democracy. But a church is not a democracy. At least it shouldn't be—despite the widely held belief of many Christians and the governmental practices of tens of thousands of churches.

This is precisely why Gateway's elder board is constituted to operate only by unanimous consent rather that by simple majority rule. A government based on majority votes will invariably become infused with politics and political maneuvering. It's unavoidable.

A democracy mind-set can seep in and poison the governmental environment in other ways. For example, it's not uncommon for various interest groups in the church to become convinced that their special agendas need representation on the elder board.

Don't get me wrong. I'm grateful we have a representative form of government in the United States in which we elect men and women to represent our views and values in the national legislature. But that is a miserable way to run a church government. Nevertheless, we live in an age of "identity politics" in which so many of us have grown accustomed to viewing ourselves primarily as members of one or more aggrieved groups who aren't getting our fair share of the pie. More and more that paradigm is leaking into the church.

Pastors or elder/deacon bodies routinely hear complaints that there is no one on the board to represent the views and needs of _____. (Fill in the blank with your choice of *singles, seniors, parents of young children, single parents, left-handed people,* and so on.)

This is why we view it as vital that elders avoid drifting into the subtle but divisive trap of politicking. In other words, an elder cannot allow himself to be viewed as a representative of the needs of any particular group or faction in the church. He can't position himself as the champion of any special interest group that may want to see change in a certain area. An elder's responsibility is to hear God for the vision, direction, and care of the congregation and then do his best to harmonize what he believes he is hearing with what the pastor and other elders are hearing from the Lord.

Certainly this may involve seeking and listening to the needs and concerns of the members of the congregation at times. But it does not mean the elder is primarily responsible for representing the needs and wants of the people. On the contrary, his responsibility is to care for them and lead them as a spokesman for the unified elder body.

It is equally vital that an elder not operate secretly or in a divisive manner outside of elders' meetings, such as calling and polling the other members to see where they stand on a matter. It can also involve taking individual elders or staff members out for lunch purely for the purpose of lobbying to build a consensus of support for a position. Such political behavior is damaging to the work of ministry.

In a similar way, a healthy elder does not operate reflexively or consistently in a posture of mistrust and skepticism. He will never be a self-appointed watchman on the wall or unilaterally take upon himself the role of God's watchdog over the church, the pastor, the finances, or any other specific area of ministry.

The spirit of a healthy elder will be one of love, faith, humility, integrity, and servanthood. When an individual elder will no longer trust and rest in God's ability to work through the combined voices of the pastor and other elders—but rather feels that he must be suspicious of others—it is a sign that his governmental mantle for this church has lifted. God does not work in division and disunity.

27

The Pastor-Elder Relationship

IN MY CONVERSATIONS WITH OTHER SENIOR PASTORS over the years, I've heard one particular anecdote repeated many times with slight variations. The story goes something like this:

> A successful businessman and his family join the church, and he immediately begins to make a positive contribution to the life of the body. He is not only a generous and faithful giver, but he also gives of his time and energy. He clearly loves the church and loves me, the pastor. I get to know him, and we build a relationship over a span of several years.
>
> It becomes increasingly clear to me that this man would make a wonderful elder for our church. He understands finance and organizational growth. And he's my biggest fan! So the day comes when I appoint him to the elder body, and suddenly this wonderful friend and supporter turns into a completely different person. Overnight my advocate becomes my adversary—questioning everything I do and challenging every initiative I propose. One day he's a labrador retriever and the next he's a pit bull.

When speaking at pastors' conferences, I have described this Jekyll and Hyde scenario and asked if any of the pastors in the room can relate to that experience. Invariably hands fly up all over the auditorium. The sad fact is, many pastors dread elder-deacon meetings. An astonishing number of pastors view these encounters as the very worst part of their role as pastor.

Why is this experience so common? There are several reasons that we'll explore shortly. But more importantly, we'll examine the ways in which our singular headship–plural leadership approach to church government has minimized the opportunities for this phenomenon and helped us nip it in the bud on the rare occasions it has tried to emerge.

One major reason for this Jekyll and Hyde revelation is that the personality and temperament traits that make for strong leaders in the corporate world and successful entrepreneurs in the marketplace can, if not fully submitted to the Holy Spirit, produce elders who try to dominate, control, and remake the church in their own image. Men who start and successfully grow their own businesses— as with those who rise to the top of the corporate ladder—overwhelming tend to be high D individuals in the language of the popular DISC temperament assessment model. In this model, the *D* stands for "Driver" or "Dominance." People whose highest scores fall into the D category are generally driven to succeed, are compelled to fix everything around them, and don't shy away from conflict in order to impose their wills. These characteristics fuel the success of these people.

In other words, the very qualities that make certain men attractive and valuable as elders can also make them a nightmare to lead. It is the reason why oftentimes a pastor finds his elder board filled with men who are fighting him and each other for control. I've often heard my friend and mentor Dr. Jack Hayford say that nearly all dysfunction in church government comes down to issues of power and control.

People who successfully grow businesses tend to be visionaries skilled at getting others to rally around their personal vision. They derive a deep sense of satisfaction from convincing others to buy into their vision and then seeing that vision become a reality.

⤳ Keys to a Blessed Church

> The very qualities that make certain men attractive and valuable as elders can also make them a nightmare to lead. It is the reason why oftentimes a senior pastor finds his elder board filled with men who are fighting him and each other for control.
>
> Who is wise and understanding among you? Let him show by good conduct that his works are done in the meekness of wisdom. (James 3:13)

Without a deliberate governmental and spiritual model that properly channels these tendencies, it's foolish to think these men will simply switch off these characteristics when they enter the church boardroom. As I've already suggested, I believe the singular headship–plural leadership approach is such a model.

That's the big picture, but what about the details? What follows are some of the key principles and practical details involved in living out this approach in real life.

THE PASTOR, ELDERSHIP, AND CHURCH ADMINISTRATION

"Good fences make good neighbors"—so the old saying goes. And there is wisdom in it. When the boundaries and lines of responsibility are clear to everyone from the beginning, the possibilities for confusion, strife, and dysfunction are greatly reduced. This is certainly true where the daily operation of the church is concerned.

At Gateway we have clear lines of authority in place regarding important matters such as administration of church staff and correction of error within the congregation. Here are a few examples of these boundaries.

Elders' Governmental Authority

As Gateway Church's government handbook describes it, "The office of Elder is a governmental office with spiritual responsibilities and rewards." Our view is that the elders have *governing* authority only when they are meeting as a group to conduct church business. In the context of the meeting, individual elders have the opportunity to speak to issues relating to the church and express opinions about the church's methods, results, and personnel. But when they walk out of the meeting room door, that governing or administrative authority falls dormant. What remains is *ministry* authority. An elder carries ministry authority at all times in all contexts relating to the church.

A specific example might help you understand this distinction. An ongoing problem with a particular staff member would likely come up for discussion in the elders' meeting. Possible solutions and courses of action would be discussed. Any elder, operating in the board's governing authority, would be free to offer a perspective or propose a solution in the meeting.

That falls clearly within the elder board's governing authority. But the execution and follow-through of the board's agreed upon course of action belongs solely to the senior pastor and the staff hierarchy working under his administrative authority. In other words, once an elder leaves the elder meeting, it would be out of bounds for him to intervene directly in that personnel problem.

Finally, a lot of churches will have elders for *spiritual* oversight but have a traditional board for the *financial* oversight of the church. I don't believe this is a healthy approach primarily because it makes an unbiblical statement—namely, that money and finance are not spiritual. Our view is that every aspect of a church's life and function is spiritual in nature. Vision (which is spiritual) must drive financial decisions. You can't do it the other way around—allowing finances to determine your vision.

Elders' Ministry Authority

What, exactly, does an elder's ministry authority entail? It certainly includes communicating the heart and vision of the leadership to the body. It involves teaching, ministering to, and exhorting the membership as well. And it certainly entails modeling and maintaining a standard of biblical behavior in the local church.

We also believe the Lord has given the elders the responsibility to provide spiritual oversight for those who join the church. This is consistent with the command of 1 Peter 5:2 to "shepherd the flock of God." Of course, we do not believe God has given the elders absolute responsibility or authority in an individual member's life, but we do believe there are three specific areas in which they are responsible for giving spiritual oversight:

1. cases of open and blatant sin (see 1 Corinthians 5:1–2)
2. issues involving doctrinal error (see 2 Peter 2:1–22)
3. divisive and contentious behavior within the congregation (see Titus 3:9–11)

In a healthy church the need for this type of intervention is rare. But when it is necessary, these confrontations must be handled biblically—in humility, with compassion, and with restoration as the objective.

We make every effort to meet with the member who requires this type of confrontation. Our desire is to help our members grow to maturity through compassionate mentoring. The biblical model of confrontation and correction is not meant to punish people but rather to protect the body of Christ from the wages of unrepentant sin. Biblical authority is not a license to exert control; it is a responsibility to exert influence for God's will to be accomplished.

Pastor's Administrative Authority

Balance! I have already described the ideal of healthy tension between the plural leadership of the elders and senior staff on one hand, and the singular, visionary headship of the senior pastor on the other. And we've just explored the prerogatives and limitations of an elder in Gateway's approach to maintaining this balance. Now allow me to say a few words about the senior pastor's part in this equation.

We believe the senior pastor should be the uncontested leader of the church on a daily basis. We also believe, however, that he functions as the representative of the corporate mind and heart of the eldership to both the staff and the congregation. In other words, the senior pastor is what connects the eldership to the people.

Of course, a healthy balance is only possible in an atmosphere of mutual honor and respect with the elder body. As the singular head of the entity, the senior pastor plays a vital role in creating that atmosphere by leading the elders regularly into the presence of the Lord through times of worship, prayer, fellowship, and impartation of his heart.

In our approach to church government, the staff and daily administration of the church is guided by the senior pastor and carried out by those to whom he delegates. The senior pastor is the singular head over the staff and the voice of the elder body to the congregation. This prevents opportunities for confusion, division, and fragmentation that result when elders have the liberty to intervene directly in the operation of the organization.

The senior pastor functions as the chairman of the elder board. I am in every sense an elder too—but a special kind of elder—one who is the chief among equals. As chairman I am responsible for preparing the agenda for meetings and then leading those meetings. It's my responsibility to see that the eldership is informed on all important issues and is aware of the current direction of the church. As I've stated previously, we make all major decisions in unanimity rather than by a mere majority vote.

At Gateway the eldership never micromanages the church or usurps the senior pastor's authority to run the church. There is a clear chain of command reflected in the church's organizational chart, and the elders never insert themselves into that chain. The elders don't dictate what I preach, but I am always eager to hear what the Holy Spirit is saying to them. And if they perceive certain widespread needs or challenges in the church body, I certainly want to hear about them.

So, what about the boundaries and limitations of the senior pastor's role? In our system of government, the senior pastor operates within clear parameters that are built into the bylaws of the church, which are periodically reviewed by the board of elders. These fences provide the senior pastor with two vital things—protection and accountability. Which are precisely what get thrown out the window when a founding pastor creates his dream scenario by packing his board with friends and relatives prone to submit to his every whim.

In our system of government, any existing elder can nominate a person for eldership, as can I. New elders must be approved by all the elders. This means if one elder knows reasons why the challenges of eldership might prove too much for the candidate, he can voice his disapproval. I'm always mindful that the wise senior pastor looks for elders that possess the qualities I've described above, rather than looking for men who are likely to go along with whatever he wants to do. I have enough sense to know that if I do that, I'm robbing myself of the protection and accountability that every fallible human being needs. And the bigger my vision and calling, the more accountability and protection I need.

In practical terms, any boundaries for the senior pastor must be broad enough to give him real authority to lead and run the church, including the authority to fill approved positions and to release personnel if needed.

Naturally, prayer should guide all decisions of both the pastor and the elder body. The bigger the decision, the more time to pray and seek the Lord should be built into the decision-making process. And valuing relationships above issues will go a long way toward keeping all debate gracious and preventing honest disagreements from becoming personal.

28

Staff, Non-Staff, and Apostolic Elders

THERE IS ONE IMPORTANT ASPECT OF GATEWAY'S APPROACH to church government that we have not yet examined. It revolves around the fact that there are three distinct types of elders sitting on Gateway's elder board. Some are members of Gateway's pastoral staff, that is, employees of the church. Others are laymen who, although they are active members of the church, are not employees of Gateway. For the purposes of clarity and brevity, I'll refer to these two respective groups as staff elders and non-staff elders. In addition, there is a third group of elders, who are neither staff nor church members—but more on them later.

STAFF AND NON-STAFF ELDERS

Over the years our approach to the elder board has evolved. Today we strive for a general balance between staff and non-staff elders on the board. But this was not the case in the beginning. In the early years of Gateway's existence, our elder board consisted of several very successful, very godly men from the world of business and finance. These were strong leaders with strong personalities.

One of these was Steve Dulin, a dear friend and brother whose wisdom and insights on eldership have been invaluable in the creation of this section of *The Blessed Church*. Steve founded and grew an enormously successful construction company. He sold that company awhile back and moved into full-time ministry.

Steve is also a frequent speaker at our pastors' conferences on the subject of effective elder boards. Here, in Steve's own words delivered at such a conference, is his perspective on how our elder board operated in those early days when we were still finding our way:

I had been really blessed in business; and in the beginning I suppose I thought that if I knew how to run a business, then I surely knew how to run a church too. I was wrong. I realize now how common and how dangerous that kind of thinking is for guys like me who run businesses.

The other men on the elder board were very accomplished in their fields as well. One was the CEO of one of the largest commercial development companies in the southwest. He routinely launched projects with price tags that ran into the hundreds of millions of dollars. Another member had owned nearly a dozen car dealerships across north Texas.

In other words, we had some pretty strong guys. And unfortunately we were kind of young at the church, and we all had our own visions for what the church ought to do and be. Counting Pastor Robert, we had at least four competing visions, and, not surprisingly, we started having some problems. At times it got ugly.

I have been asked by people who know I've been at Gateway from the very beginning if we ever had any problems or rough patches from a leadership standpoint. My answer is, "Oh yes, we had to work through some problems."

A lot of the stress and pressure came because we were experiencing such tremendous growth. The growth brought challenges. And each of us thought we had the best ideas about how to address those challenges.

So you may be wondering, *What happened?* Well, here's what happened: Tom Lane came. Tom Lane became Gateway's executive senior pastor (Robert's Number Two) and joined the elder board. Tom came in, and he was such a stabilizing influence. Tom came in with a fatherly influence and experience running a big church. Of course, we know-it-all business guys immediately started challenging him and butting heads with him. But Tom was so wise in the way he worked with us.

Tom and Robert arranged for us all to go on what we called a guided sabbatical. It was a retreat in which, for the very first time, we really got to know each other. We elders thought we knew each other, but we didn't. It was amazing what we found out about each other. And it brought us such stability and harmony. We've really been on an upward path ever since. We started walking in unity, walking in relationship, and having the same vision. God has blessed that.

Now we take elders retreats twice each year. It is out of all this that our principle of "Relationships above issues" was birthed.

There are some important truths in the above excerpt that I want to high-light and elaborate upon. Namely, it is clear to me now as I look back on those early years that I had a lot to learn about leading an elder board—and as the senior pastor, it is my job to lead. Steve mentioned that we frequently had four different, competing visions for the church. That's a prescription for paralysis. God, in His grace and mercy, didn't allow our lack of understanding to hurt the growth and general health of the church body in that season. Eventually, the Lord showed all of us the kind of order I have laid out in the preceding chapters. Namely, that vision can only come through one person, and that person must be the senior pastor.

Another reason we were out of balance in our early years is that non-staff people from the worlds of business and finance comprised almost our entire elder board. As Steve referenced in his talk, our first staff elder with relevant church-running experience was Tom Lane. Since that time we have added several other senior staff pastors to the elder board—as we have felt appropriate—based upon their character, spirit, and gifting.

Don't misunderstand me. This wasn't about loading the elder board with people more likely to see things my way—remember, we don't operate by majority vote. We move in unanimous agreement, or we don't move at all. Rather, we have learned the value of having a general balance of staff and non-staff elders on the board, although we are not rigidly committed to a perfect fifty-fifty split. I have discovered there is enormous value in having both types of perspective—from inside and outside the organization.

❧ Keys to a Blessed Church

> There is wisdom in having a general balance of staff and non-staff elders on the board. There is enormous value in having both types of perspective—from inside and outside the organization.
>
> > Counsel in the heart of man is like deep water,
> > But a man of understanding will draw it out.
> > (Proverbs 20:5)

There are two special roles, however, that have been reserved for the non-staff elders for very practical reasons. One relates to my compensation. Since I am the organizational executive that oversees all staff, it would be awkward and unseemly for them to participate in setting my compensation. Since I'm involved in setting their salaries, it would create an apparent conflict of interests if they in turn could set mine. That's why the non-staff elders function as an executive compensation subcommittee in our system. They utilize all the best comparative charts and nationwide compensation surveys to ensure that we are well within the boundaries looked upon favorably by the Internal Revenue Service.

Second, two of our non-staff elders have the special assignment to look after me. Steve Dulin, the non-staff elder I quoted extensively above, and Gayland Lawshe are commissioned by God and permissioned by me to monitor my physical, spiritual, and emotional well-being as well as that of my family. They have become a priceless source of real and meaningful accountability for me.

At regular intervals Steve, Gayland, and I will meet for lunch or coffee, and I'll hear questions like:

- "So, how are you doing? Really?"
- "Are you getting enough rest? exercise?"
- "How's your relationship with Debbie? When was the last time you had a date night?"
- "How are your stress levels?"
- "Are you delegating what can be delegated so you can concentrate on the things only you can do?"
- "How much are you traveling? How many speaking invitations are you accepting each month?"
- "Let us see your calendar!"

Here is how Steve described his role (it's from the same presentation I quoted above):

> If the senior pastor is not healthy, it's really hard for the church to be healthy. And I believe my number one concern and responsibility at Gateway Church is the health and well-being of Pastor Robert and his family. This is my burden. My main job is to make sure he and his family are encouraged, strengthened, blessed, protected, and taken care of. My job is not to make sure Pastor Robert doesn't make any mistakes. That's the job of the Holy Spirit. My job is to help protect him. To hold up his arms, to be a shield for him. That's my job. That's my burden. That's the calling that I have.

This is accountability and care. Every senior pastor needs it. (But sadly, not every pastor wants it.) However, a member of the senior pastor's staff is not really in a position to provide it. This is a role ideally suited for a non-staff elder, but he has to be called to it. It requires an extraordinary level of transparency on the senior pastor's part, which means an extraordinary level of trust in that elder is essential.

APOSTOLIC ELDERS

A third type of elder plays a key role in Gateway's approach to government. This type of elder is neither a full-time staff member nor a member of the church at all. Allow me to explain.

I am a passionate believer that the local church should be autonomous and free to serve the community in the way it best sees fit. Nevertheless, there are times in the life of a church when authoritative, trusted, objective input from outside is critical to the life and health of the church. We have come up with a fancy, official-sounding word for this role—*translocal accountability*—but I prefer the term *apostolic elder.*

An apostolic elder is a mutually agreed upon source of counsel and mediation should some sort of deadlock form within the elder body. In my view, both the senior pastor and eldership should agree in advance on who should fulfill this role for the church.

You will recall that Jimmy Evans of Trinity Fellowship Church in Amarillo fulfilled a key role in the planting of Gateway Church. So it was natural for us to turn to him to be our first and lead apostolic elder. Dr. Jack Hayford and James Robison fill significant roles in the life of our body as well, and they also graciously fill the role of apostolic elders for us. They, like Jimmy, are universally respected and honored. Their integrity, knowledge of the Word, and ability to hear the voice of the Holy Spirit are unquestioned. All three men understand my vision and love our church. These qualities make these men ideally suited for the role of what the Bible calls an *overseer* (see Acts 20:28; 1 Peter 5:2).

In fact, this role is actually written into our bylaws, which state that if the elders have an issue that we can't resolve, our appeal is to our apostolic elders and their decision is final!

Why do we designate such an elder as *apostolic*? Well, first and foremost we believe the office of apostle is alive and well here on earth. I'm sure you're very familiar with the five ministry gifts to the church listed in Ephesians:

> And He Himself gave some to be apostles, some prophets, some evange-
> lists, and some pastors and teachers, for the equipping of the saints for
> the work of ministry, for the edifying of the body of Christ, till we all
> come to the unity of the faith and of the knowledge of the Son of God,
> to a perfect man, to the measure of the stature of the fullness of Christ.
> (4:11–13)

I'm equally sure you know that the Greek word *apostolos* literally means, "a delegate, a messenger, or one who is sent forth with orders." In church history, the role of apostle has been viewed as a church planter or church overseer. But as it is used in the New Testament, there is the additional meaning of "one who sets things in order." This is exactly the role the apostle Paul assumed in 1 Corinthians 11:34 when he corrected the Corinthian church about their abuses of the communion table: "But if anyone is hungry, let him eat at home, lest you come together for judgment. And *the rest I will set in order when I come.*"

He was going to come and set things in order...because that's what apostles do.

Because our approach to church government stipulates that we move forward only when we're in unanimity, there is always the possibility that we could find ourselves at an impasse. It's extraordinarily rare, but it's possible.

It's rare because our approach also calls for us to prize relationships above issues and to pray and worship together regularly. This leads to an atmosphere of trust and a mutual respect in each member's ability to hear from the Spirit of the Lord. It's also rare in practice because in most circumstances, if eight members of the elder body feel one way and one member is unsure, he will ordinarily defer to the other members and say, "Hey, I trust you guys. More importantly, I trust the Holy Spirit in you."

If, on the other hand, one or more dissenting members continue to feel strongly—even after an additional season of prayer and seeking the Lord—a decision point is reached. The group can decide to simply set aside the initiative or project because unanimity hasn't been reached. But what if the majority feels equally strongly that the project is of God? At that point the group might agree to call in one of the apostolic elders to speak into the situation.

For Gateway, this has not been necessary very often. But when it has been necessary, we've never failed to come to a resolution that everyone has confidence in, and it has allowed us to move forward together in unity and peace.

The wrong church government is a box that limits our growth and causes tremendous pain. The right government is a solid and stable foundation that allows us to build God's house as large and as fruitful as He desires!

PART 6

Blessed Church Culture

29

The Power of Culture

Who are we? What's important around here? What are we known for? What characterizes our people, our plans, and our passion? Who sticks to us like glue? Whom do we repel?

These are questions of culture. An organization's culture is not so much about *what* it does but *how* it goes about doing it. Culture is about values, attitudes, priorities, and paradigms. And every organization—from global corporations to single-parent households—has a culture. So does your church, whether you recognize it or not.

We shouldn't be afraid to learn about the power of culture from the world of business. Apple is widely known for cultivating a culture of innovation and creativity. Nordstrom department stores were long known for instilling a culture of extraordinary customer service. And Southwest Airlines is famous for its culture of fun and is rewarded with consistently high marks from both employees and customers as a result.

Of course, organizational culture can and does work in the negative as well. For example, some believe it was Enron's culture of risk taking and overconfidence that led to one of the most spectacular corporate collapses in US history.

Culture is a product of leadership. It flows from the top down and from the inside out. This is as true for churches as it is for corporations. What determines your specific culture as a church? It is a product of what you, as a leader, emphasize, teach, model, measure, fund, celebrate, reward, and punish. Having a church culture is not optional. You *will* have one. You can either be intentional and purpose driven about what kind of culture you create, or you can just let "what will be will be."

⁓§ Keys to a Blessed Church

> Your specific culture as a church is a product of what you, as a leader, emphasize, teach, model, measure, fund, celebrate, reward, and punish.
>
> > The things which you learned and received and heard and saw in me, these do, and the God of peace will be with you. (Philippians 4:9)

At Gateway we chose to be intentional. We took a hard look at what we believed God had called us to do, and then we took inventory of our God-given passions. Of course, we measured all in the light of Scripture and the principles we found there. What emerged was a clear picture of what we would look like if we were doing and being all that God had placed in my heart.

In our case, it meant finding ways to cultivate some key attributes and attitudes throughout the organization. There are many, but five of these in particular stand out as helping to define who we are as a church. We purposed to have:

- a culture of generosity (stewardship)
- a culture of freedom
- a culture of rest (Sabbath honoring)
- a culture of worship
- a culture of community

On the pages that follow, I'll expand on the meaning of these phrases and share some insights regarding how the Lord helped us build a culture that embodies these values.

30

A Culture of Generosity

TEN YEARS AGO I PUBLISHED MY FIRST BOOK, *The Blessed Life*. In it I shared a remarkable journey God had taken Debbie and me on as a couple. It was our wild, exciting adventure into radical stewardship, extravagant giving, joy, and miraculous provision. In it, I also explained a lot of what God had taught me over the years about how to properly relate to wealth and possessions. In other words, I wrote a book about how to be bless-able.

What happened next took me by surprise. Actually it floored me. *The Blessed Life* struck a chord with hundreds of thousands of people all over the world. In its first year—without a publisher to champion, distribute, or promote it—tens of thousands of copies sold. Then we started getting requests for two hundred, three hundred, a thousand, even three thousand copies at a time. It turned out that many pastors read it and then wanted every family in their churches to have a copy. Today churches from a variety of denominations hand a copy of *The Blessed Life* to every one of their new members.

Why?

Because good pastors love their people and want to see them blessed! That's certainly my heart for the people I have the privilege to pastor at Gateway. I want them to experience that adventure too. I want to help them live lives of blessing, purpose, peace, and eternal impact for God. I want them to know what makes them bless-able.

Making that dream a reality requires one thing: cultivating a culture of stewardship. At Gateway Church the Lord has blessed us with some success in achieving that goal. I've had numerous outsiders remark to me that Gateway is one of the most generous, giving congregations they've ever witnessed.

What's different about our approach? The most distinctive aspect is that we rejected what has become the most common strategy for getting people to give. I'm talking about the giving-to-get message that has become the default paradigm in recent years.

When Debbie and I were first starting out, we adopted a lifestyle of generosity because we were immensely grateful to God for saving us and because He had birthed in our hearts a genuine desire to help people—not because we were looking for a great return on investment for our money.

LIVE IT

This is the first vital key to creating a culture of stewardship in your church. You first have to *live it*.

We have taught our staff and our people what we've personally experienced…that giving is a joy in and of itself, that it's an act of worship, and that it's the one act that makes us most like our heavenly Father. Does God bless generosity and obedience? Of course! But we've consistently taught our people that this blessing should be seen as the by-product, rather than the motivation, for giving. We teach that it's all about the heart. And we teach that the blessings that do tend to result from sharing of our material possessions are not all financial. True blessing encompasses every area of our lives.

I teach it the way I learned it. If you've read *The Blessed Life,* you know that Debbie and I began by tithing. I know tithing is biblical and powerful and God honoring so I teach it unapologetically. To our practice of tithing we added a lifestyle of giving to people and to ministries as the Holy Spirit led us. That has sometimes required giving courageously, extravagantly, even radically. Not to boast but to illustrate—we've given away more than fifteen vehicles in our married life and one house. On more than one occasion, we've cleaned out our savings and retirement accounts in order to obey a prompting from the Lord.

Of course, our faithful God has always restored us abundantly. But the point is that it was fun. Holding with an open hand everything God has entrusted to you is an exciting adventure.

✑ Keys to a Blessed Church

> We've consistently taught our people that blessing should be seen as the by-product, rather than the motivation, for giving. We teach that it's all about the heart.
>
>> For the LORD does not see as man sees; for man looks at the outward appearance, but the LORD looks at the heart. (1 Samuel 16:7)

I share all this because we have operated Gateway Church this same way from the very beginning. I believe God knows He can trust us with resources, because we've demonstrated that we will distribute them as He directs. This is the root of a culture of stewardship and generosity. What other things have we done to create this culture?

PREACH IT

The second is fairly obvious: I preach on it. But I'm diligent to do so with the right motive. As I stated, God is interested in our hearts, and this is no less true for us pastors. Ask yourself, *What's my motive for preaching on giving?* That's not as easy of a question to answer as you might think. The reason is that when you're examining your own heart, the Enemy is quick to whisper some condemning suggestions. He'll say, *You're only teaching this because you want the church to have more money. You're being greedy. You're materialistic.*

This is precisely why many pastors are ineffective in preaching about money—if they preach about it at all. They're conflicted, and that conflict robs them of boldness and authority.

When I encounter a pastor who is wrestling with this kind of conflict, I ask him a series of questions. The conversation usually goes something like this:

"Do you ever preach about marriage and family?"

"Of course!"

"And if you were about to preach a series on marriage and family, what would your motive be?"

"It would be to help people, of course. I want them to understand the spiritual principles and truths that make for great marriages and healthy families."

"But wait a moment. Won't your church be stronger, bigger, and more effective if the marriages are strong and the families are healthy?"

"Absolutely."

"Then aren't you being selfish and self-serving by preaching on these things?

"No! My motives are pure. I know these truths will help people in an area in which the Enemy is constantly attacking."

Do you see it? This is precisely what the Enemy does to us when it comes to preaching about finances and stewardship. But because it concerns money rather than marriage, we let him get away with it.

What is true about God's principles for families is true of His principles of stewardship. Understanding God's way of thinking about and handling finances will help our flock. It will improve their lives and their kingdom effectiveness in an area in which the Enemy is very prone to attack them.

Then make that your motive and preach it boldly—the same way you preach about grace, salvation, walking in forgiveness, or any of the other vital truths of Scripture.

By the way, one of the reasons that we have as many divorces among Christians as we do is that preachers don't preach on giving. Why are these things linked? It is because giving is the subject that deals most directly with the issue of selfishness in the heart. There is a direct string from the wallet to the heart. In Matthew 6:21, Jesus declared that "where your treasure is, there your heart will be also." A lot of pastors misquote that. They say, "You know where your heart is...there your treasure will be."

That's not what Jesus said. Your treasure doesn't follow your heart. Your heart follows your treasure. Invest a chunk of your hard-earned savings in a particular stock, then watch and see if you don't start checking on it two or three times a day to see how it's doing.

Don't let selfish people determine what you preach. The people that get mad when you preach on stewardship are invariably the nongivers. Let them leave if it comes to that. Yes, people with selfish hearts need to be given ample opportunity to soften and change. But if they don't, you'll be healthier without them. Do what I do. When someone comes up to me and says, "Pastor, it bothers me when you preach on money. It makes me uncomfortable," I respond with, "Well, the Holy Spirit instructs me about what to preach so you'll need to take that up with Him."

Do you want to help your people? (If you have a shepherd's heart, I know you do.) Then get them to put their treasure in the church. In practical terms, I preach a stewardship-centric series normally every two years. But I'm also diligent to take opportunities to make points about stewardship and generosity in other messages—at least once each month.

Why? Because selfishness is poison to the Christian. Nothing is more opposed to the spirit of Jesus and the heart of God. And nothing propels a believer into maturity and effectiveness in God's kingdom faster than learning to be unselfish. And it is impossible to put a dagger through the heart of selfishness in people's lives without teaching them to think like *stewards* rather than *owners*.

Selfish people break their marriage vows. Selfish people cause problems in the church—sowing strife, division, and discord. Selfish people produce broken, wounded, selfish kids. When you address selfishness from the pulpit, you save marriages. Most importantly, selfish people will never fulfill their destiny and calling in God. You owe it to your people to teach them to live a lifestyle of generosity and stewardship. And teaching on this periodically is a major key to creating a culture of generosity in your church.

In your teaching, it is vital to view successful stewards in your church properly and to teach others to do the same. Many of the wealthiest people in our church are very generous givers to the kingdom—not just by virtue of the *amounts* they give but also by the *percentages* of their incomes they give away. This is no coincidence. They didn't become generous after they grew wealthy; rather, they grew wealthy because they were generous. There is a very successful businessman in our congregation who for years has been giving away more than fifty percent of his annual income. And he began this practice long before his income was substantial. And yet he has a problem. The more millions of dollars he gives away, the more God gives him to exercise stewardship over. He's been trying to outgive God for years, and he just keeps falling farther and farther behind in the race. And he's not the only one.

One day I was driving with a visitor from out of town, and we happened to pass by the house of one of our wealthier members. It's a lovely house. I mentioned that it belonged to one of our members, and this gentlemen's instant response was, "He ought to sell that and give the money to the poor." Of course, my immediate thought was, *Isn't that exactly what Judas said about the perfumed anointing oil that was poured upon Jesus?* The comment bothered me because he was talking about one of the most generous people I have ever known. So I said, "Why don't you sell *your* house and give the money to the poor if you're so concerned about them? I'm sure you live like a king compared to the way most of the people on this planet live."

This person had judged my friend solely because he was wealthy. Many pastors do the same thing from the pulpit. They make subtle and not-so-subtle comments that communicate their belief that wealthy people are inherently evil and that having financial success is something they should apologize for and feel some shame about. Believers who have experienced remarkable success can have a difficult time finding a Bible-believing church that doesn't treat them like either lepers or slot machines that might pay off big if the right lever gets pulled.

Many people have observed that Gateway Church has a large number of very wealthy individuals as members. It's true, I suppose. But this is only because we have deliberately created a culture that doesn't treat them differently from the way we treat everyone else.

Heeding the warnings of James 2:2–4, we don't treat wealthy members as if they belong to a better class of human being. But we don't view them as sinful by virtue of their success either. We keep Jesus's observation of the widow's mite ever in mind—recognizing that with God it is about the sacrifice involved in the gift and the intention of the heart of the giver. I've watched families with household incomes of thirty thousand dollars make much more extravagant gifts than those with six-figure incomes. And vice versa!

MODEL IT

The third key to creating a stewardship culture in your church is to model it. You have to build it from the top down. That means it must start with the senior pastor, extend to the staff, and on to the lay leadership before it can be embraced by the membership. As Jesus said in Luke 16:11, "Therefore if you have not been faithful in the unrighteous mammon, who will commit to your trust the true riches?"

This saying applies to us as pastors as much or more than to anyone. If you haven't been faithful with your own money, why would God give you people? People are the "true riches." I'm convinced that a major reason God has seen fit to grow Gateway so radically and rapidly is that we've demonstrated that we are good stewards with "unrighteous mammon." As a result, He has entrusted us with the true riches of people to disciple and equip.

Modeling stewardship is different from living it. Of course, you can't model it if you're not living it. But by modeling it, I mean sharing truths with the congregation by using personal illustrations and anecdotes.

I share my stewardship mistakes. I share my failures and how God redeems them. I share my breakthroughs and blessings. And invariably, these are the things people find most memorable. God uses my stories and my experiences to impart truth and principles.

We operate the finances of the church the same way we operate our own finances. This can best be summed up in three short phrases. We *spend wisely, save aggressively,* and *give generously!*

31

A Culture of Freedom

"It was for freedom that Christ set us free." So says Galatians 5:1 (NASB). I believe much of the church has grossly underestimated the depth and breadth of that freedom Jesus died to purchase for us. Yes, in Christ we have been freed from the curse of going to hell when we die. This is the ultimate deliverance. And, certainly, we have been freed from sin's yoke of guilt and shame in this life. Yet there are dimensions of freedom that I believe many believers and their pastors have overlooked.

The very fact that Paul reminded us that it was to enable us to enjoy a lifestyle of freedom that Jesus purchased our freedom tells us something important: It lets us know that it is possible to fail to walk in all the freedom that belongs to us—that it is possible to fall back into bondage. In fact, the second half of Galatians 5:1 warns us of this very thing:

> Stand fast therefore in the liberty by which Christ has made us free,
> *and do not be entangled again with a yoke of bondage.*

The Bible explicitly declares two objectives of Jesus's earthly ministry: His mission "to seek and to save that which was lost" (Luke 19:10) and to "destroy the works of the devil" (1 John 3:8).

Of course, as pastors we have a front-row seat to observe the works of the devil in our day. These works shackle even born-again, Jesus-loving people to unhealthy life habits, patterns of destructive behavior, and cycles of defeat. Yes, there are physical and mental components to many of these addictions, compulsions, and bondages. But there is a clear and real spiritual component too. It's often called a demonic stronghold.

Can believers have demonic strongholds in their lives? I know they can for two reasons: the Word indicates it, and I've personally experienced it. So have all of the mentors, colleagues, and co-laboring ministers I most respect. We have all had to come to grips with the fact that just because we're born again, well-acquainted with God's Word, and even called to full-time ministry doesn't mean we're automatically going to walk in all of the freedom Jesus died to provide. In fact, achieving and maintaining freedom requires attention, effort, and vigilance.

Please understand that I'm not referring to believers as being demon possessed. We must first realize that any time we read the term *demon possessed* in English, it is not the term used in the original languages of Scripture. Two common terms in the Greek *daimonion echei,* translated "has a demon" (John 10:20), and *daimonizomenou* (John 10:21), are best understood as "demonized." In neither case in the original language is there a suggestion of "possession." In fact, in the case of the first phrase, the implication is just the opposite: the spirit does not have the person; the person has the spirit.

✑ Keys to a Blessed Church

Just because we're born again, well-acquainted with God's Word, and even called to full-time ministry doesn't mean we're automatically going to walk in all of the freedom Jesus died to provide. In fact, achieving and maintaining freedom requires attention, effort, and vigilance.

Stand fast therefore in the liberty by which Christ has made us free, and do not be entangled again with a yoke of bondage. (Galatians 5:1)

The terms Jesus used when speaking of the presence of demonic forces in individuals clearly imply that the spirits were issued forth *from within*—as opposed to around, beside, or near—the person. For example we find *ap' autou,* meaning "off or out of the self," in Matthew 17:18. We see *ekblēthentos*—"plucked out and expelled from within" in Matthew 9:33. And the term *ex-elthontos*—"to issue forth from"—is used in Luke 11:14. These phrases would indicate an internal position of influence much like a bacterial or viral infection inside the body.

These declarations of Jesus reveal His understanding of demons' ability to influence people. And what about believers? Our clearest scriptural example is found in 2 Corinthians 12:7 (NASB) where Paul stated, "Because of the surpassing greatness of the revelations, for this reason, to keep me from exalting myself, there was given me a thorn in the flesh, a messenger of Satan to torment me— to keep me from exalting myself!"

Here Paul said a "messenger of Satan" (*angelos*) had been sent to be a thorn in his "flesh" (*sarki*). These phrases suggest that an angel of Satan, also known as a demon, was afflicting his physical person.

In my experience, demonic forces can influence a person in varying degrees from both outside and from within. The body and the soul (mind, will, and emotions) can provide a haven for influencing spirits if the door is opened to them. The spirit of a born-again believer has been made alive and sealed by the Holy Spirit of God (see John 6:63; Ephesians 2:1–5; 1 Peter 3:18), but as Paul made clear, we can either live by the flesh or live by the Spirit. According to Ephesians 4:26–27, when we live by the flesh, we give the devil an opportunity (*topos*—a place or geographical location).

Why is all this important? Because as ministers we will never achieve the levels of effectiveness and impact to which we're called if we're held in bondage by the Enemy in certain compartments of our lives. And we can't lead God's people in freedom if we're not modeling a lifestyle of liberty ourselves.

This is why cultivating a culture of freedom is a high priority at Gateway

Church and why we are passionate about helping people get and stay free. We model and teach the kind of life and activities that allow people not only to obtain freedom but also to maintain and expand it in their lives.

The kinds of activities that we consider important to help in these areas include educating people regarding their identity in Christ and the fullness of life available to them, engaging their wills in the process, helping them wage spiritual warfare for themselves and their loved ones, and gaining an ability to recognize and eliminate what led to their bondage in the first place.

At Gateway we call it Freedom Ministry, and we've worked deliberately to remove any stigma or shame associated with it. I talk openly and regularly to the staff and the congregation about how I avail myself of freedom ministry as needed. And we are transparent and accountable to each other about our struggles and weaknesses.

At the same time, we're diligent not to get weird or unbalanced where these things are concerned. We endeavor to maintain a healthy balance between the extremes by discerning and responding with authority to strongholds and demonic spirits, while helping individuals recognize and accept their own responsibility for life choices. To put it simply, we need deliverance *and* discipleship. As my good friend Pastor Jack Hayford says, "You can't disciple a demon, and you can't cast out the flesh!"

Our focus is based on core values anchored in Scripture that help us maintain this balance as we minister freedom to individuals. The values that help us cultivate a culture of freedom include the following:

- *A Commitment to Biblical Foundations* (see 2 Timothy 3:16): To maintain the health of our Freedom Ministry, we consider Scripture as our foundation for all we do. All experience will be screened through our understanding of Scripture.
- *Being Solution-Focused* (see Philippians 4:8): We will make Jesus, His work, and the work of the Holy Spirit more prominent than the work of unclean spirits.

- *Being Spirit-Guided* (see John 5:19): We will develop our ears
  for the guiding voice of God so that we may do what we see
  the Father doing.
- *Operating in Compassion* (see 2 Timothy 2:24): We will treat
  people with the love and compassion which have been shown
  to us. We will treat God's children the way we would want our
  children to be treated.
- *The Fruit of the Spirit* (see Galatians 5:22–23): We will conduct
  ourselves and our ministry in a way that reflects the fruit of the
  Spirit.
- *Facilitating Discipleship* (see Ephesians 4:16): We are
  growing disciples with long-term fruit and the ability to
  reproduce.
- *Facilitating Personal Growth* (see Matthew 10:8): We are not
  teaching techniques; we are passing on what we have freely
  received.
- *Promoting Unity* (see Psalm 133:1): We are stronger together
  than we are as individuals. We will accept and grow from one
  another's differences.

Our Freedom Ministry seeks to embody Jesus's mission to undo the works of the devil in our own lives, in the lives of our pastors and staff, and in the lives of our members. We desire to help people grow in their souls (mind, will, emotions) through elements of teaching and discipleship so that they can grow in freedom as they seek to know and serve Jesus Christ.

We also work to make compassionate ministry settings available for groups and individuals so that people can encounter God in the areas of their need.

We love to help people be free. To do that, we know we must follow Jesus's model and instruct people regarding kingdom life. We must also help them encounter our living and present God who acts in power and authority to overcome the impact of living in a fallen world. Such an encounter is designed to help people break free from strongholds and demonic oppression in their lives, allowing God's people to live fully as His redeemed sons and daughters.

And that brings us to our next cultural goal as an organization.

32

A Culture of Rest

FROM THE OPENING LINES OF THIS BOOK, I have tried to make it clear that Gateway Church is far from perfect. We don't have all the answers. And we're not walking perfectly or consistently in all that we do. In other words, for every principle of church health and growth that I have put forth here, there can be a gap between what we *want* and *hope* and *endeavor* to do, and what we are *actually doing.*

There are areas in which the gap between our ideals and our performance is blessedly small on most days. In other areas, we have some work to do to get a closer alignment between our practice and our principles. In no area do we have a greater struggle to close the gap than in the one we call the principle of rest (sometimes referred to as the principle of the Sabbath).

We believe in it. We know it's vital. We have systems and policies and safeguards to help apply the principle across the organization. And yet I would be less than transparent if I didn't tell you that we're not quite where we want to be. Allow me to explain the principle, and perhaps you'll begin to see why it can be such a battle to come into alignment with when your church is doubling in size every few years.

I'm sure I don't have to tell you that life in full-time ministry can be exhausting—physically, emotionally, and spiritually. Church work is infamous for chewing good people up and spitting them out. This can be the case under any circumstances but is doubly true when a church is growing rapidly. An extended season of vigorous growth is exciting, but it can also put a huge strain on all resources—especially the human ones.

Organizational and individual health doesn't happen by accident. Without a deliberate plan to keep everyone balanced, everyone involved—from the senior pastor on down—is in danger of falling victim to something I call shrunken heart syndrome.

Just as posttraumatic stress disorder can be debilitating for soldiers who have served on the front lines of combat, shrunken heart syndrome is a condition that affects many who serve on the front lines of ministry. The key symptoms include diminished or missing compassion, a loss of empathy, and a general loss of the emotional energy that makes effective ministry to others possible.

Factors that contribute to the onset of shrunken heart syndrome include

- no speed bumps for schedule demands (reflexively saying yes to everything)
- no margin (pushing past the limit via a well-intentioned drive to produce results)
- no Sabbath (ignoring the principle of rest)
- no replenishing relationships (focusing on results rather than people)
- no governor on growth (enabling a system that permits chronic shortages in infrastructure and resources)

Does any of that sound familiar? When Gateway started growing like crazy, it became clear that we were going to have to put some biblically based, Holy Spirit–inspired systems and safeguards in place if we were going to avoid completely burning out me and everyone else in the ministry. I'm so thankful to the Lord that we did. The ten-plus year trajectory of hypergrowth we've experienced would have been unsustainable if the Lord had not led us to directly address the issues of rest, relationships, and recovery.

Out of those early efforts emerged these precepts:

- a commitment to principles—especially the principle of the Sabbath rest
- clearly defined and protected priorities

- a radical, problem-solving mind-set
- replenishing activities and relationships

THE SABBATH REST

First of all, this principle isn't about whether the Lord prefers to be worshiped on Saturday or Sunday. I'm certainly aware that there are people who feel very strongly about that question and that whole denominations have been formed and split over the issue. I'm referring to the principle we find in the book of Exodus:

> Remember the Sabbath day, to keep it holy. Six days you shall labor and do all your work, but the seventh day is the Sabbath of the LORD your God. In it you shall do no work: you, nor your son, nor your daughter, nor your male servant, nor your female servant, nor your cattle, nor your stranger who is within your gates. For in six days the LORD made the heavens and the earth, the sea, and all that is in them, and rested the seventh day. Therefore the LORD blessed the Sabbath day and hallowed it. (20:8–11)

Behind every Old Testament law lies an eternal principle. Every commandment, every Levitical decree—even the most obscure priestly regulation—is either an expression of some everlasting truth about how to live a life of blessing and divine purpose, or it points us by types, symbols, and shadows to a New Covenant fulfillment in Jesus Christ and His kingdom. Or both!

This is certainly the case with the principle of the Sabbath. This book is not the place for a thorough examination of the Sabbath as it applies to the believer today. Let it suffice to say that at Gateway we take the principle of rest seriously and know that we neglect it at the risk of our health, well-being, and effectiveness in the kingdom.

We have a staff filled with pastors and Christian professionals who are passionate about their callings and driven to deliver excellence in everything they do. The demands that ministry puts on me and everyone around me—in every part of the organization—are breathtaking. That's why I quickly learned that *as an organization* we must think and act intentionally about the Sabbath. What we have endeavored—and are still endeavoring—to do is cultivate a culture of rest. Like everything else, I know that establishment of this value begins with me.

✑ Keys to a Blessed Church

Organizational and individual health doesn't happen by accident. Without a deliberate plan to keep everyone balanced, all involved—from the senior pastor on down—are in danger of falling victim to shrunken heart syndrome.

> If you turn away your foot from the Sabbath,
> From doing your pleasure on My holy day,
> And call the Sabbath a delight,
> The holy day of the LORD honorable,
> And shall honor Him, not doing your own ways,
> Nor finding your own pleasure,
> Nor speaking your own words,
> Then you shall delight yourself in the LORD;
> And I will cause you to ride on the high hills of the
>   earth,
> And feed you with the heritage of Jacob your father.
> The mouth of the LORD has spoken. (Isaiah 58:13–14)

In chapter 28, I mentioned how two of the non-staff members of our elder body have the assignment of looking after my physical, emotional, and spiritual health. A key part of that role for them is holding me accountable where rest is concerned. This accountability includes making sure I'm following our established sabbatical schedule.

Our rest policy requires that every fifth year the senior pastor take an eight-week-long sabbatical. I did precisely that on my fifth anniversary, but when I hit my tenth anniversary the elders came to me with a surprising directive. After seeking the Lord and praying, the consensus was that for this milestone sabbatical I was to take not eight weeks off, but twelve. They were quite firm about it.

I wondered if the church could really afford for me to be away from the pulpit for that long. (I don't think I'm the only pastor who has a little of him that wants to believe everything will fall apart if he's not there.) But the elders insisted and I submitted. (Actually, it wasn't that hard to submit.) As with my other sabbaticals, my strict instructions were to completely unplug from the day-to-day business of the church—no e-mail, no cell phone calls...no cheating! I was to devote my time solely to fellowship with the Lord, enjoying my wife and family, and relaxing.

It was wonderful, but I couldn't help but wonder from time to time how the church was faring. Then about a week before the sabbatical was scheduled to end, Steve Dulin, one of the elders assigned to look after my health and well-being, stopped by for a visit. He said, "Well, Robert, I have good news, and I have good news. Which do you want first."

I liked the sound of that. I replied, "Give me the good news first!"

Steve said, "Well, over the last few months, attendance is up and giving is up!"

"And the other good news?"

"We're giving you another month off!"

He was kidding about that second thing, of course. And to be honest, no one was more thrilled than I to learn that the church had prospered in my absence. I didn't view it as a sign I wasn't needed. I saw it as evidence that God was building something at Gateway that wasn't dependent upon one man. The fact that our attendance and giving actually went up while I was gone was a glorious confirmation that God blesses us when we are intentional about following His direction for our lives.

We also have a sabbatical policy in place for all our pastoral staff. And Gateway's emphasis on healthy staff families is reflected in the commitment of each staff member to not work more than fifty hours per week and not more than three nights a week, to have two days off a week, and to use all allotted vacation time each year. We talk about these requirements when we make a new hire, and we have systems in place to help see that they are followed.

Nevertheless, it is ultimately the responsibility of each individual pastor and staff member to honor the principle of rest. We can't force our people to do so any more than we can force them to maintain a good attitude. At the same time, it is our desire to establish and maintain a culture of rest by giving priority to the principle of the Sabbath. This is necessary even if pastoral duties fill the weekends. For some of us our day of rest falls on Monday. For others, it's Friday.

The principle of Sabbath is to cease from labor. Whatever you do at work, don't do on your Sabbath! If you're a surgeon, don't operate on anyone! If you're in construction, don't build anything! If you're in ministry, don't write a message, work on a book, take a counseling appointment, answer e-mails, tweet, or anything else you would normally do that is associated with your job!

What things should make up a Sabbath rest and be reflected in a culture of rest? Among them are:
- spending time thinking, reflecting, and creating
- celebrating God—His sovereignty, His work, His bigness
- numbering our days by prioritizing our work and other interests
- allowing accountability without drifting into legalism
- practicing the presence of God in all we do
- re-creating activities—fun, fellowship, and relationships

I like the way author and fellow senior pastor Mark Buchanan described the power of the Sabbath rest in his book *The Rest of God:*

Without rest, we miss the rest of God: the rest he invites us to enter more fully so that we might know him more deeply.... Sabbath is both a day and an attitude to nurture such stillness. It is both time on a calendar and a disposition of the heart. It is a day we enter, but just as much a way we see. Sabbath imparts the rest of God—actual physical, mental, spiritual rest, but also the *rest* of God—the things of God's nature and presence we miss in our busyness.

We have to be intentional and passionate about nurturing a culture of rest. And honoring the principle of the Sabbath is the key.

33

A Culture of Worship

As I shared the story of Gateway's founding in the opening section of this book, I mentioned that one of the things driving my sense of holy discontent (to again borrow Bill Hybels's phrase) was a desire to approach corporate worship differently from the way it was conducted by many churches I had attended.

Let me reiterate—there was nothing *wrong* with the way it was done at other fellowships. On the contrary, many times it was rich and Spirit led, and it regularly ushered God's people into a transformative encounter in the Father's presence. But there were some things about it that were not consistent with the approach to doing church I knew I was called to create, as well as the kind of worshipers I knew I was called to attract and equip.

Indeed, worship was one of the five things on which the Lord directly instructed me to focus as we prepared to launch Gateway. Please understand, I'm not using the term *worship* as a euphemism for the singing portion of our worship services—although worship certainly happens then. Worship is any activity—individual or corporate—that causes us to encounter the presence of God. And in those encounters, God is blessed and we're changed.

Obviously, the broadest and most visible manifestation of a church's worship is the corporate worship that takes place during services. But if you're going to create a culture of worship within the church—which is our goal—it must extend to every aspect of the church body.

Why is this so vital? Because, in my view, church is not about *observing* God. It is not learning facts *about* God. It is about *experiencing* God. And it is impossible to experience God—individually or corporately—without worship. As Psalm 100 reminds us, we "enter into His gates with thanksgiving, and into His courts with praise" (verse 4).

This is why we begin every elders meeting with a season of worship. Before we make a single decision and before we discuss a single item of business, one of our worship pastors joins us to lead us in thirty minutes to an hour of prayer and worship. Why? Because we need to hear God! Yes, we're all busy. Yes, our time is precious. But that is precisely why we can't afford *not* to take the time necessary to experience the presence of God. Making poor decisions wastes both time and money. In fact, with kingdom work, poor decisions can cost lives and affect eternal destinies. What we do in these meetings is too serious and too consequential to too many people to undertake it without God and His will front and center.

You may recall the account in Second Kings in which King Jehoram visited the prophet Elisha because he needed to determine the will of the Lord. The king basically said, "Hey prophet, I need you to hear God for me." And Elisha's response was, "Bring me a musician" (3:15).

> Then it happened, when the musician played, that the hand of the LORD
> came upon him. And he said, "Thus says the LORD: 'Make this valley
> full of ditches.' For thus says the LORD: 'You shall not see wind, nor shall
> you see rain; yet that valley shall be filled with water, so that you, your
> cattle, and your animals may drink.' And this is a simple matter in the
> sight of the LORD; He will also deliver the Moabites into your hand."
> (2 Kings 3:15–18)

Even Elisha—the one who had received a double portion of the mighty anointing that rested upon Elijah—needed to experience worship before he could access the wisdom and counsel of God.

We have learned to follow Elisha's example. We want to hear the voice of the Lord, so we bring in a musician to lead us into God's presence through worship.

Invariably, we're more sensitive to the Lord's voice and direction when we're finished. We're also far less likely to engage in arguments or pride-fueled disputes. You see, it's really difficult to be selfish or act out of the flesh when the God of the Universe has just manifested Himself in your midst.

This approach of putting a priority on worship extends beyond our elders' meetings into every facet of the ministry—from small groups to children's classes to fishing retreats in the men's ministry.

Still, the cornerstone of any church's worship life is found in its weekend service or services. When we launched Gateway Church, I didn't know a lot, but I knew with certainty that we were going to do two things at the very highest level of our ability. (Note that I didn't say "better than everyone else." Just to the best of *our* ability.) Those two things were feeding the sheep (preaching), and leading the sheep into the presence of God (corporate worship).

We strove for excellence in both of these areas from the outset—and I mean excellence in every sense of the word. I have already shared my convictions about the need for God-honoring technical excellence and skill. And an individual having the right heart, calling, and anointing is vital—indispensable. But all of these things are enhanced and refined through diligent, hard work.

I won't apologize for wanting our worship to be delivered with skill and talent, but we never want to fall into the trap of thinking we're putting on a show. So strong is our conviction that we must not view what we do as *performing* that we don't allow the platform to be called "the stage." A stage is for performing. A platform is for influence!

Worship is not a show. And if we start thinking that the key to attracting and holding people is by putting on a better show than the world offers, we're in trouble.

Have you seen a Broadway play, a blockbuster movie, or a concert lately? We're never going to have a better show than the world does, because they can spend fifty million dollars on it. Attempting to deliver a Sunday morning worship experience that is a bigger production than Saturday night's movie is a foolish and fruitless endeavor.

It is not about our performance. It's about His presence. Excellence is lifeless if God doesn't show up. And no matter how good our "show" is, people can always find a church down the street that puts on a better one. Church is not about *exhibiting* God. It's about meeting with God. It's about *experiencing* God!

We have succeeded when a spiritually hungry person walks into one of our services for the very first time and then leaves saying, "I felt something. I don't even know how to describe it, but I know I'll be back next week."

⇜§ Keys to a Blessed Church

Worship is not a show. And if we start thinking that the key to attracting and holding people is by putting on a better show than the world offers, we're in trouble.

But the hour is coming, and now is, when the true worshipers will worship the Father in spirit and truth; for the Father is seeking such to worship Him. (John 4:23)

A HOUSE OF GOD

Genesis 28 is a special passage for us at Gateway. As I explained in chapter 2, it contains the verse the Lord used to give me the very name of our church—verse 17. The sermon I preached on our very first Sunday centered on this chapter. And in it we find a key truth that is a cornerstone of how we have been led to do church.

As I'm sure you know, this passage describes Jacob's life-altering encounter with the presence of God at Bethel. Here in the wilderness between Beersheba and Haran, Jacob had stopped for the night and placed a stone at his head as a pillow. There was symbolic significance in this act of placing the stone under his head. As we discover as the passage unfolds, this head stone or chief stone would later become a holy memorial pillar.

As he slept, Jacob dreamed he saw a ladder connecting earth to heaven, with angels ascending and descending on it. Then Jacob heard the Lord speaking to him—making some amazing promises and predictions about Jacob's calling and future.

> Then Jacob awoke from his sleep and said, "Surely the LORD is in this place, and I did not know it." And he was afraid and said, "How awesome is this place! This is none other than the house of God, and this is the gate of heaven!" (Genesis 28:16–17)

The structure of that first sentence is a little grammatically odd—with the first half of it in the present tense and the second half expressed in the past. But the Lord wrote it just the way He wanted it. It may be bad grammar, but it's great theology. Jacob is essentially saying, "The Lord is here right now. In fact, He has been in this place all along, but I wasn't aware of it until this moment."

Like Jacob prior to his dream, it is possible to be in the presence of the Lord and be utterly unaware of it. It happens in churches all over the world every weekend.

I recall attending a pastor's conference several years ago and having an open vision during the worship portion of a service. As we were singing, I felt a very strong sense of God's presence in the place. Suddenly I saw Jesus walk in through one of the doors at the back of the sanctuary. He was going from person to person, embracing them in a hug, putting His hands upon them—blessing them and loving on them. But then I noticed that He would walk up to some people, and they would not respond to Him. They just stood there singing. Jesus would wait a while for them to engage Him, but eventually He would just move on to another person.

I realized that I was seeing something that very accurately reflected what was taking place in the room as we worshiped. Most were aware of the Lord's presence in the place and were being changed and blessed as a result—just as Jacob was transformed when he became aware of God's presence. But some— even in a group of pastors—were too distracted or preoccupied to notice that the One we were singing about had walked into the room carrying a blessing.

The name Bethel (literally Beth-El) means "House of God." Or put another way, it's a house in which God's presence can be found. That's what *church* should be. And it is precisely what we have consistently prayed, worked, and pressed to be over the years. We want to make people aware of the presence of God, because we know that when that happens, wonderful things follow—for them and for everyone around them.

CULTIVATING A WORSHIP CULTURE

We believe God has called Gateway worship to help create highly influential God worshipers. Simply put, we believe God has called all of us as priests to minister to God and to each other, regardless of whether we are a congregational member or a platform musician/vocalist. Worship, we believe, is a lifestyle, and as we walk in this lifestyle, we will impact our families, our neighborhoods, and eventually our world.

In our worship ministry, we focus on five foundational values from the outset:

- *Core*—our understanding of worship
- *Character*—our relationship with Jesus
- *Craft*—our talent or gifting
- *Community*—our relationship as a family
- *Chemistry*—our connection with the congregation and with God

We focus on these areas through various opportunities and classes. We offer Equip classes (both live and via video) throughout the year that educate our membership in the theology of worship. Throughout the year, we offer various levels of training for certain instruments or team positions. As people get involved in our family, we focus on encouraging their relationship with the Lord through our relationship with them. We make every effort to connect relationally with those involved in our ministry, and we communicate in word and deed what it looks like to be a priest who connects others to God.

We are not perfect at this, of course. But I'm blessed to know that every week we're helping people experience transformative encounters with the presence of God—and not just in our primary worship services. It's happening in living rooms where our small groups meet, in children's church, at breakfasts for business people, and in scores of other contexts.

Nothing blesses me more because, as a pastor, I know that when we connect intimately with Him and hear His voice, more of His character and nature will emerge in us.

34

A Culture of Community

THE IDEA OF UTILIZING SMALL GROUPS TO FOSTER relationships and connectedness in a church body is not a new one. The number of books written on this
theme over the last twenty years would probably fill a warehouse.

There is a reason for this. A sense of belonging to a community is one of the
deepest and most fundamental human needs. Yet we live in a day in which community is harder and harder to build. It's a time of increasing isolation and dis-
connectedness; today people are less likely to even *know,* much less interact with,
their neighbors. To the degree that relationships exist, they tend to be superficial
and fleeting. And some recent studies have shown that social-media technologies
like Facebook create the illusion of connectedness without actually providing
any of the vital depth and meaning found in real relationships.

Of course, if any place this side of heaven should offer a sense of community
and connectedness, it should be our churches. There people are joined not just
by cords of natural relationship but also by supernatural ties that make us all
part of the same body. We're not just friends; we're family:

> Therefore, as we have opportunity, let us do good to all, especially
> to those who are of the household of faith. (Galatians 6:10)

> Both the one who makes men holy and those who are made holy are
> of the same family. So Jesus is not ashamed to call them brothers.
> (Hebrews 2:11, NIV)

And yet in the modern era, churches have struggled in this area—as the mountain of books with the phrases *cell church, small groups,* and *life groups* in the titles attests. This is doubly challenging when the church is growing rapidly.

THE ESSENCE OF COMMUNITY: SMALL GROUPS

For all of these reasons, from the very beginning we have been committed to creating a sense of connectedness for every member of Gateway Church. As with many other churches, small groups are the cornerstone of our strategy on this front. But at the core of our approach is a philosophy I described back in chapter 17, "Who's the Minister Here?" Namely, we don't view my primary role or the role of the other staff pastors as ministering to our people. Our goal is to *equip* them to minister—to each other and to a hurting world. Our small groups are the training and practice ground for that ministry.

Would it surprise you to learn that out of all the facets of our ministry at Gateway Church—including worship services that attract tens of thousands each weekend—the one responsible for seeing the most people come to Christ each year is our small-groups ministry? That's right, the most evangelistic thing we do happens, for the most part, in living rooms.

That is no happy accident. It is the fruit of a strategy. For example, we pay to provide free child care for the vast majority of the hundreds of Gateway small groups that meet each week. This is a significant expense, but it removes a huge barrier to participation for many and even provides a powerful incentive for some—especially extremely busy and stressed single moms.

Think about it. If most of our salvations are happening in our small groups, that means that the people having the wonderful privilege of leading others to Christ are our members, rather than our pastors.

This is the very model of ministry we find in the electrifying first days of the church as recorded in the book of Acts—with ministry happening in homes and frequently being carried out by Holy Spirit-infused lay people:

So continuing daily with one accord in the temple, and breaking bread from house to house, they ate their food with gladness and simplicity of heart. (2:46)

And daily in the temple, and in every house, they did not cease teaching and preaching Jesus as the Christ. (5:42)

Of course, evangelism isn't the only kind of ministry happening in our small groups. They are by design safe, nurturing places for believers to learn to do the greater works of Jesus (see John 14:12). In the early days, our small groups were almost exclusively home groups structured around discussing the previous weekend's message along with time for worship, sharing of needs and victories, and prayer. Today we have an astonishing array of group types and contexts. Some are Bible studies. Others are prayer groups. Some coalesce around a special interest or need. We have small groups for owners of small businesses, for people with a passion to pray for the nations, for single parents, and so forth.

We have a very popular, wonderfully fruitful subset of groups called T2, built around the exhortation of Titus 2:3–4, for older women to disciple the younger women in the church. In these groups, mature women (spiritually and in age) share their wisdom and insights in a context that makes them mentors to newly married ladies and young mothers.

HOW WE ENCOURAGE A CULTURE OF COMMUNITY

Before we could really be intentional about fostering community at Gateway Church, we had to decide what we meant when we used the term *community*.

We decided that, for us, community is characterized by

- a group of people wherein you are known and find relationship
- a group wherein you know people and serve their needs

- a group made up of people with common values and interests and who do life together
- a connection that makes people feel they belong and matter
- relational commitment, not task or vision

We decided that if we were going to build a culture of community we needed to identify *where* people are in the process of connecting and help them move to the next step of community connection. We had to find ways to help them move from superficial and convenient connections to relationships that are intentional and committed—relationships that provide genuine care and meaningful accountability.

We defined four levels of community involvement, presented in order here from most superficial to deepest and most rewarding:

- *Facade*—This is the entry level of community and the entry point to relationship with others. It's the least demanding and least intimidating.
- *Facilitator*—This is the starting point for connection. Here we work to identify people's needs or their desires for a place to belong, and then we facilitate meeting the need or desire.
- *Friend*—This is someone with whom you have social contact, know personally, and have some level of thoughtful interaction.
- *Family*—This is the deepest level of connection; it's based on relationship, involvement, and commitment.

Of course, the shallower your relationships, the more of them you can have. Relationally it's possible to be a mile wide and a half-inch deep. This is especially true in a large church. A person in the Facade level of community involvement can have an almost unlimited number of relationships, because they are all nothing more than casual acquaintances and familiar faces. Such a person may pitch in to help with something the church is doing from time to time, but there is no commitment and no continuity to that involvement. If this person suddenly stops attending, it is very possible that no one will notice.

✑ Keys to a Blessed Church

Of course, the shallower your relationships, the more of them you can have. Relationally, it's possible to be a mile wide and a half-inch deep. This is especially true in a large church.

That their hearts may be encouraged, being knit together in love, and attaining to all riches of the full assurance of understanding, to the knowledge of the mystery of God, both of the Father and of Christ. (Colossians 2:2)

We've estimated that a person who has moved on to the Facilitator level can maintain between two hundred and four hundred relationships. A person at this level feels more obligated to help others and does so more consistently. They are also more likely to feel some sense of responsibility toward others coupled with a compassionate desire to see people at the Facade level get better connected. Ideally, the connections with some of these people will deepen, and this person will move into the Friend level of community.

At the Friend level, a person really *knows* others and is known by them. There is real commitment to the things in which this person is involved. Because the relationships at this level are deeper, they are by necessity fewer in number. We estimate a Friend has between one and two hundred relationships.

Finally, the highest, deepest level of community is the Family level. When you are connected at this level, you have somewhere between ten to fifty people who really know you and are known by you. You can count on each other to be there in times of trouble or pain. Galatians 6:2 happens in this level: "Bear one another's burdens, and so fulfill the law of Christ." Hebrews 10:24–25 happens here too: "And let us consider one another in order to stir up love and good works, not forsaking the assembling of ourselves together, as is the manner of some, but exhorting one another, and so much the more as you see the Day approaching."

When you're in the Family level of community and you suddenly stop attending church, it will definitely be noticed! Other members will take it upon themselves to find out where you are and how you're doing.

With any church, but especially a church the size of ours, it's possible to attend for months or even years without ever connecting. With these levels in mind, we have tried to design systems that encourage and enable people to move through these layers of community rather than remaining on the periphery.

We talk community regularly. We emphasize it periodically. And, perhaps most importantly, as in the case of providing free child care for those attending small groups, we put our budget where our mouth is.

All of these things help move us ever closer to our goal of creating a culture of community.

Conclusion

WELL, THERE YOU HAVE IT. AT THE OUTSET I PROMISED to explain not *what* Gateway does, but *why* we do what we do. In other words, I wanted to present to you, in all humility and gratitude, the principles, purposes, and passions that have driven our decisions since founding Gateway Church back in the year 2000. This I have done as well as I can.

As I close, I need you to know that if you're a pastor or church leader, I'm cheering for you. I want your church to be robust, vibrant, and healthy—knowing that if you can achieve health, growth will be a natural result. And growth for your church means more people saved; more believers discipled; more priests equipped for ministry; more sharing of the redemptive, restorative, transformative love of God in the workplace and marketplace.

I know it may sound trite, but we really are playing for the same team. In the battle for souls on planet Earth, we'll win together. I am reminded of what Paul said:

> Now he who plants and he who waters are one, and each one will receive his own reward according to his own labor. For we are God's fellow workers; you are God's field, you are God's building. According to the grace of God which was given to me, as a wise master builder I have laid the foundation, and another builds on it. But let each one take heed how he builds on it. (1 Corinthians 3:8–10)

God's fellow workers! That's quite an honor for you and me. We are builders with God. And if we're going to build the church, then like Paul, we must become wise master builders. I believe there are four key characteristics to that kind of church builder.

First, wise master builders build according to a blueprint. They don't wing it. You'll recall that God told Moses to build according to the pattern he'd been shown (see Exodus 25:40). Just as God gave Moses a pattern for building the tabernacle, He has given us in Scripture a pattern for building the church.

I once talked with a sincere young preacher who said, "I want to build a church that focuses exclusively on the next generation." My response? I said, "Well, that's great but that's not a church. That's a youth ministry." Youth ministry focuses on the next generation, and there's nothing wrong with being called to youth ministry. It's a noble calling. But a *church* focuses on all generations, all cultures, all races, and both genders. That's part of the pattern. A church can have a youth ministry, but a youth ministry can't be a church.

We are called to be the builders, not the architects. The plans have already been drawn. This is what troubles me about some of the books, conferences, and seminars on church reinvention today. It's as if we're bored with the pattern and feel compelled to come up with a new one. I'm not against learning new methods, but I am against adopting a new mandate, which has been the same for nearly two thousand years: go make disciples!

We're living in a world of increasing specialization. Everything from jobs to kitchen utensils are more specialized. Where there used to be three or four television channels, we now have four hundred—with a specialized channel for every niche and interest you can possibly imagine. Coffee used to come two ways— regular and decaf. Now it takes a flow chart and an iPad app to decide what you're going to drink.

Don't get me wrong. I'm not a crotchety old geezer grousing about all these newfangled contraptions that are messing everything up. I like change in things that can be improved. But there is no improving God's pattern for what a church is and does. Yes, we can modernize our methods. (At Gateway, we have!) Certainly we can harness the power of new technologies to deliver biblical truth and life to people. (We do!) But what we can never move away from is our understanding that Jesus came to found an *ecclesia*—a diverse gathering.

⤦ Keys to a Blessed Church

> We are called to be the builders, not the architects. The plans have already been drawn. We can never move away from our understanding that Jesus came to found an *ecclesia*—a diverse gathering.
>
> > Having been built on the foundation of the apostles and prophets, Jesus Christ Himself being the chief cornerstone, in whom the whole building, being fitted together, grows into a holy temple in the Lord, in whom you also are being built together for a dwelling place of God in the Spirit. (Ephesians 2:20–22)

In an age characterized by specialization and customization, we're assured that the key to marketing is to find a niche. Pastors take that advice to heart and decide their church is going to specialize in something. And I've heard the range of specialties:

"We specialize in reaching the lost."

"We're going after the unchurched."

"We're called to speak to millennials."

"We're going to focus on missions."

"We're going to major in compassion for the poor and oppressed."

The fact is, all of those things are wonderful and spring directly from the heart of God, and they are *all* part of our mission. But from that extraordinary day the Holy Spirit was poured out upon a diverse group of one hundred twenty people gathered (*ecclesia*) in the Upper Room up until to today as you hold this book in your hands, being the church has meant gathering "whosoever will," equipping them for ministry, and displaying to the culture a full-color, 3-D, panoramic picture of Jesus to a lost world.

As Paul explained in Ephesians, Jesus has presented the church with five presents—five ministry gifts—and He gave them for a specific purpose, until a specific goal is reached:

> And He Himself gave some to be apostles, some prophets, some evange-
> lists, and some pastors and teachers, for the equipping of the saints for
> the work of ministry, for the edifying of the body of Christ, till we all
> come to the unity of the faith and of the knowledge of the Son of God,
> to a perfect man, to the measure of the stature of the fullness of Christ.
> (4:11–13)

As wise master builders, we don't get to choose the kind of house we're building.

Now I do think the Lord lets us pick the flooring and the paint on the house that we are building (to carry the metaphor further), but we can't change the rooms included. The Architect plans direct that you have to have a kitchen—you have to feed people. You have to have a living room too. You have to provide a place for God's people to commune with Him. This isn't optional. You must build bedrooms—places for them to find rest from the battle.

Yes, God's heart is to reach the lost and the unchurched, but as I've stated repeatedly, I believe with all my heart that God's plan for doing that is to equip His people to share their faith out there—in the workplace, at the PTA meeting, and in the grocery store aisle.

In the very first new-members class we ever held at Gateway, someone asked me, "Do you have a strategy for evangelism and church growth?"

My answer was, "Yes. Our strategy is, 'Feed the sheep.'" Healthy, strong sheep reach people.

That brings me to the second characteristic of wise master builders: they build with quality. By this I mean we build high-quality believers. We build people who represent the very best of what a follower of Jesus Christ can be. I don't have to remind you that your church is not your building. Your church is your people (actually *His* people). Therefore the quality of the church you are building is defined by the quality of the people you equip.

We take great care to never forget that building people is what we're called to do. Again, it's why our rallying cry from the beginning has been "We're all about people." Be a quality builder!

Thirdly, wise master builders build with love. I've known quite a few home builders through the years, and the very best among them did their work with great passion. They loved the process. They loved the outcome. They loved putting families in homes. In the same way, the best churches I know are pastored by people who love building up people.

May I urge you with all sincerity, if you've lost your love for people, take a break! Go on a sabbatical; reconnect with the heart of God, and find out how it can be expressed through His calling on your life. Don't simply keep trudging along and going through the motions. Remain a pastor, rather than a CEO who preaches. You can't be a wise master builder if you've lost your passion for God's people.

Finally, a wise master builder must also learn to build and fight at the same time. I don't have to tell you that we're in a war. Satan would love to take you out. He's playing for keeps. We've seen that, haven't we? We've seen men and women who really love God get taken out by some trap or scheme of the Enemy.

We have to be like Nehemiah and his men who carried a construction tool in one hand and a weapon in the other (see Nehemiah 4:17). This is essentially what successful pastoring and leadership involves.

This is why everyone on our staff has a team of intercessors who pray for us regularly. It's actually a requirement of being on our pastoral staff: you have to handpick a team of seasoned, fervent pray-ers.

Let's also guard ourselves against being critical of those who fall. As Paul said in Romans 14:4, "Who are you to judge another's servant?" And consider Galatians 6:1: "Brethren, if a man is overtaken in any trespass, you who are spiritual restore such a one in a spirit of gentleness, considering yourself lest you also be tempted." They are God's building. They are God's field. We're all God's fellow workers.

A FINAL WORD OF ENCOURAGEMENT

I strive to be a wise master builder. I endeavor to be ever mindful that I'm building something that doesn't belong to me—I'm just the steward. I haven't arrived. I fall short in many areas. But we serve a patient and merciful God.

That's why I want to close by encouraging you not to get discouraged. Of all the weapons the Enemy wields against pastors, I think discouragement is the most prevalent and most lethal. You don't grow a crop in a day. You don't build a house in a day either. It takes time.

Regarding all the work and prayer and planning and hardship you've suffered to follow the call upon your life, allow me to point you to the words of the Holy Spirit expressed through the writer of Hebrews:

> For God is not unjust to forget your work and labor of love which you
> have shown toward His name, in that you have ministered to the saints,
> and do minister. (6:10)

And remember the words of Galatians:

> And let us not grow weary while doing good, for in due season we shall
> reap if we do not lose heart. (6:9)

I felt strongly as I was finishing this thought that the above verse might be an encouraging word from the Lord for you.

Press in. Press on. And together let's build blessed people. Let's build a blessed church. Here's my prayer for you:

Lord, I pray that You would take the truth of Your Word and cause it to sink deeply into our hearts. Lord, I pray for all the builders—that You would give us grace and power to be Wise Master Builders. I lift up the shepherds of Your flock—that You would place in us the heart of The True Shepherd.

Lord, I ask You to bless and strengthen all those who have said "Yes" to Your high call to serve Your people and to reach those who have not yet accepted You. Pour Your life and light into the work of their hands. We ask for blessed churches for the building of Your kingdom and for Your glory.

In Jesus's name,

Amen

Acknowledgments

I want to say thank you to the members, volunteers, staff, and elders of Gateway Church. Without you, this book would not have been possible. It's an honor to serve the Lord with you.

And to David Holland, my faithful friend and co-laborer in this book and several others, thank you for helping me put into words the principles God put in my heart.